Environmental Economics:

A Simple Introduction

Also by K.H. Erickson

Simple Introductions

Accounting and Finance Formulas
Applied Econometrics
Choice Theory
Corporate Finance Formulas
eBay
Econometrics
Economics
Environmental Economics
Financial Economics
Financial Risk Management
Game Theory
Game Theory for Business
International Relations
Investment Appraisal
Investment Formulas
Marketing Management Concepts and Tools
Mathematical Formulas for Economics and Business
Methods of Microeconomics
Microeconomics

Environmental Economics:

A Simple Introduction

K.H. Erickson

Contents

1 Introduction

Environmental economics applies established economic principles of equilibrium, market failure, efficiency, and valuation techniques to environmental issues. In doing so environmental economics can understand the incentives causing pollution and environmental degradation, and highlight the best methods to use to control them. It can reveal the most efficient use of precious natural resources so that they are not overexploited or wasted. And it can enable the advantages and disadvantages of environmental planning proposals to be valued and compared, so that the best choice of action may be calculated and then followed.

This book is divided into four parts, exploring the main areas which make up environmental economics using established theory, diagrams, equations, and examples. The first area is probably the topic most people think of when imagining environmental issues, and it is the issue of pollution or environmental degradation in a more general sense. The seemingly inevitable link between economic activity and consumption, with pollution and environmental degradation, is put forward and illustrated with a simple example. From there the question of why the market doesn't automatically resolve the pollution problem is answered, as the idea of environmental externalities and market failure is put forward. The difference between private goods and environmental public goods is explained, and public goods are revealed to allow polluters to avoid taking responsibility for the full costs of their pollution.

The solution to the pollution problem is to make polluters take responsibility for all of the costs associated with their activity, known as the Polluters Pay Principle, and several sections explore a variety of possible methods to achieve this goal in detail. Bargaining between the polluters and their victims has the potential to bring about an efficient outcome where the costs and benefits of pollution are balanced, but only if the conditions of the Coase Theorem are met. If bargaining isn't a feasible solution then government intervention may be required, and a Command and Control Policy sees quantitative and qualitative rules being set to limit pollution, yet it is an inefficient method to reduce pollution as it doesn't follow the equimarginal principle. A Pigovian Tax issued by government does follow this principle, and is therefore cost efficient, but several equity related issues are noted with the instrument. Tradable Emissions Permits are another cost efficient market based pollution control tool, but there may be problems associated with the setting up of such a system. Finally a section on pollution control analysis compares the major emission control instruments, using the criteria of static efficiency, dynamic efficiency, equity and income distribution, and performance under uncertainty.

Efficient Environmental Management is the third area to be examined, as the challenge to make optimal use of natural resources is analysed. First, renewable natural resources are investigated, as resource growth rates, stock levels, harvest sizes and harvesting effort are assessed to determine the optimal levels. And property rights or the lack of them is found to determine whether profit maximization, or the tragedy of the commons, comes to pass with renewable natural resources. Next, non-renewable natural resources such as fossil fuels are assessed, using the Hotelling rule and the modified Hotelling rule, as the resource price path, the discount rate, and extraction costs come together to create an optimal extraction rate and resource allocation over time.

The fourth and final area of the book looks into how environmental projects are valued and assessed for economic efficiency. Cost-Benefit Analysis is explained with its six steps looked at in turn, and policy valuation techniques are detailed, including stated preference, revealed preference, and production function approaches.

2 Environmental Degradation

2.1 The Pollution Problem

Every day huge amounts of harmful substances are released into the environment all across the globe. It's not that people worldwide all enjoy polluting the environment, it's that they feel they have no other choice. Whether it is the fossil fuel power stations required to generate power releasing harmful gases in developed countries, or the livestock needed for meat and dairy products releasing damaging gases through cow flatulence in rural areas and developing countries, human economic activity goes hand in hand with pollution. And it is not just big industry or farmers who are to blame as every individual consumer also leaves a trail of pollution in their wake. Every time they make a journey in their car harmful pollution is emitted from the car exhaust, and the rubbish, refuse and waste which every consumer generates ends up dumped in a landfill site, causing environmental degradation to land and sea which threatens the complex natural ecosystem.

A basic trade-off could be said to exist between economic activity and related consumption on one side, and pollution and related environmental degradation on the other side. Greater consumption is linked with greater environmental degradation, and reduced environmental quality. The following diagram shows this idea in visual form, with the dashed line showing a production possibilities frontier (PPF) representing different possible combinations of consumption levels and the resulting environmental quality levels. A move up the vertical y axis, with greater consumption, clearly sees the dashed PPF line move leftwards along the horizontal x axis, to signal reduced environmental quality.

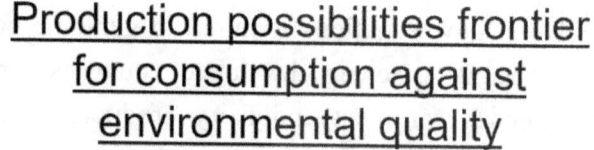

Production possibilities frontier for consumption against environmental quality

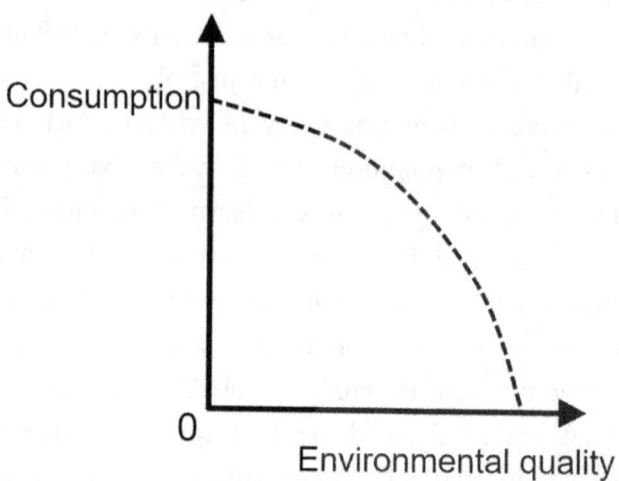

In this example diagram the production possibilities frontier is curved inwards, suggesting that the negative effects of consumption on environmental quality increases in impact as consumption reaches higher levels. This is represented by the PPF curve becoming more horizontal as consumption increases in level, at which point even a small rise in consumption (movement up in the diagram) causes huge and devastating falls in environmental quality (movement left in the diagram). The inwardly curved PPF here may be considered to be a pessimistic view of environmental preservation, but it is perhaps the most realistic. Damage to the environment can throw the whole ecosystem out of its natural state and lead to climate change, which in turn results in rising sea levels, the extinction of important creatures in the food chain, and highly erratic weather patterns, which in turn causes even greater damage to the environment.

Other possible but less likely relationships between consumption and environmental quality are a constant relationship between the two (with a straight line production possibilities frontier), or a situation where the negative effects of consumption on environmental quality decreases in impact with higher consumption levels (with an outwardly curved PPF curve). Climate change sceptics may believe the latter scenario, and they may argue that the environment will naturally adapt to deal with the pollution challenges it faces over time.

Although most people acknowledge that the reduction in environment quality caused by mass consumption and the resulting environmental degradation is a bad thing, it is difficult to stop. We have all become accustomed to a certain level of living standards and consumption, and willingly going back to a pre-industrial time and set of living standards simply isn't going to happen. However, most will also agree that we can't allow the environmental quality to be reduced to zero, and we simply can't survive without environmental resources. Therefore in practice consumption and environmental quality must be balanced, with the ideal level of each above zero.

The next diagram replicates the previous image of a production possibilities frontier with combinations of consumption and the resulting environmental quality, but in this diagram specific points have been marked. Point A on the dashed PPF curve is associated with consumption (C) of level C1, and environmental quality (Eq) at level Eq1, and in this hypothetical example it may represent the optimal combination of consumption and environmental quality. At point A consumption is relatively low to ensure the environment is mostly protected, and environmental quality is quite high and not overly degraded, but consumption is still high enough to give people a satisfactory standard of living. However, there is another point labelled on the dashed PPF, point B with a higher consumption (C) level at C2, and lower environmental quality (Eq) level at Eq2. And the presence of this second point B in the diagram highlights the nature of the pollution problem. Even if a desired combination of economic activity and consumption against pollution and environmental degradation was identified, such as point A, it is unlikely to remain a stable equilibrium. There is a tendency for consumption and related pollution to continue beyond what is desired and to a highly problematic level, such as point B in the diagram, as we can see in the real world today with the issue of climate change. The causes of this market failure to control pollution are examined and explained in the next section.

The trend toward rising consumption, and falling environmental quality

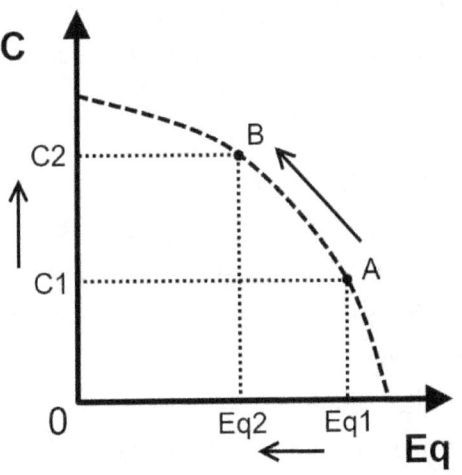

2.2 Environmental Externalities and Market Failure

The last section highlighted the fact that pollution and environmental degradation are a problem, driven by excess human economic activity and consumption. And that even if everyone agrees that pollution is a problem there is still a tendency for it to get worse and worse, causing ever greater environmental degradation. This may seem like a hard to explain result for those with a basic familiarity of economics, who have been told about market forces, the laws of supply and demand, and an expected long-run efficient equilibrium where supply equals demand. According to this basic economic theory the quantity supplied of something (e.g. a pollution causing good or service) should eventually match the quantity demanded for that same thing (e.g. a pollution causing good or service), following a process of short-run movements in the price and quantity supplied/demanded of that thing until this stable outcome is reached.

If demand is below supply, and supply is above demand, then there is excess supply or a surplus of the product. Basic economic theory would suggest that the price of the good or service is too high. It would predict that the supplier would lower the price of their product to stimulate higher demand, causing demand to rise until it matches supply, at which point the supplier will no longer be faced with an excess supply of products and will stop discounting the price of their products. This results in a stable long-run equilibrium outcome where demand equals supply.

If supply is below demand, and demand is above supply, there is excess demand or a shortage of the product. Basic economic theory would suggest that the price of the product is too low. Theory would predict that those consumers most eager to get their hands on the limited availability product would raise the price they are willing to pay, and this would give suppliers reason to supply additional units of the product and raise supply until it matched demand. At that point there would be no need for consumers to offer over the odds prices to acquire the product as there would be enough to go around, and without those higher prices and excess demand from consumers there would be no incentive for suppliers to keep raising supply. The result is a stable long-run equilibrium where supply equals demand.

The following diagram shows the economic theory that supply will equal demand in the long-run in visual form. The downward sloping demand curve, where a lower price increases the quantity of a product demanded, and upward sloping supply curve, where a higher quantity supplied increases the cost price, cross and are equal at point X. At this point the price of the product is equilibrium price Pe, and the quantity supplied/demanded of the product is equilibrium quantity Qe.

Demand and supply equilibrium

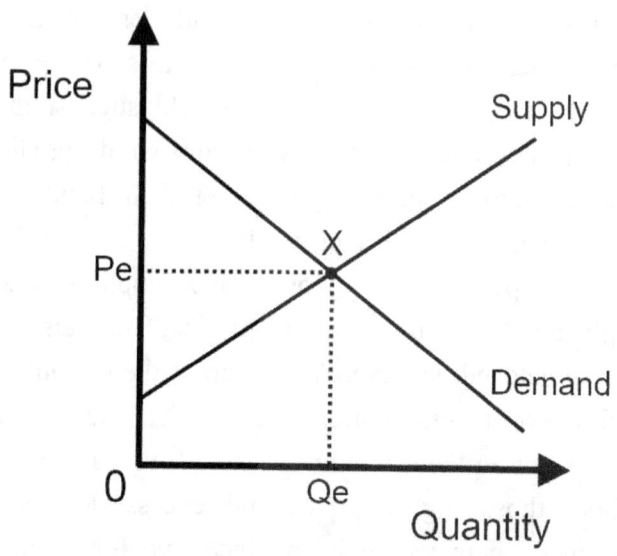

But this economic theory that supply equals demand in the long-run often doesn't hold with the issue of environmental degradation, and the demand for pollution causing activity is often far less than the supply of the pollution causing activity which actually comes to pass. Contemporary climate change makes this all too clear. And the reason the basic model above often doesn't work with environmental issues is that it ignores a vital feature of the environment which simply doesn't apply to basic man-made physical goods: the lack of property rights.

While physical goods are private goods with private property rights, following the just stated principle of the law of supply and demand, no-one holds property rights over environment features such as air or the ecosystem, and they can't be dealt with in the same way. Air and the ecosystem are instead examples of public goods, and public goods have two distinct characteristics: they are non-rival and they are non-excludable. Non-rival means that one person using the resource doesn't affect the amount available to others (the opposite of rival private physical goods), while non-excludable means that no-one can be prevented from using the resource. And these two characteristics of environmental public goods such as air and the ecosystem allow pollution to devastate and degrade them with little resistance.

With a typical man-made product the interaction between the producer and the consumer is very simple. The producer holds the property rights but is willing to transfer them over to a consumer if they receive an acceptable price for a quantity of their goods. In other words they will supply their product if there is enough demand. With a pollution causing activity this interaction also exists but there is also a second dimension which no-one agreed to, known as externalities, and made possible by the limited property rights agents hold over the environment. The name externalities stems from them being 'external' to any contract or compensation between supplying and demanding agents, and the key feature of externalities is that they do not require an agreement between the supplier/producer/seller and the demanding party/consumer/buyer, but can affect one party in an unintended way. Externalities can be either good or bad, but in the case of a pollution causing activity externalities are most definitely bad, coming in the form of pollution.

The non-excludable nature of air and the ecosystem means that pollution externalities can't be excluded from ruining someone's local air and ecosystem, whether they agreed to it or not. And non-excludability also allows the polluter to 'freeride' off other clean air and well-functioning ecosystems despite not contributing to their upkeep. The non-rival nature of air and the ecosystem also serves to compound this problem, as no matter how much damage is done the harmful effects of polluted air and a polluted ecosystem won't be used up and absorbed away, but can instead continue on damaging people's health, animals' lives, and the natural environment.

The existence of externalities in environmental issues changes the basic supply and demand diagram shown earlier. The long-run equilibrium point X where supply crosses demand still remains, with equilibrium price Pe and equilibrium quantity supplied/demanded at Qe, but due to the existence of externalities this equilibrium outcome is missed. The reason it is missed is because with environmental externalities present the supply curve comes in two parts instead of the usual one: a private supply curve with the expected supply (output) of a product, and an unexpected supply curve representing externalities (the pollution associated with that output). And with agents having no control over externalities, the forces of supply and demand must work with only the private supply curve, creating a stable expected long-run outcome where private supply equals demand.

The above description may sound complicated, and the situation can be explained far more simply with another image. In the following diagram the basic supply and demand diagram earlier has been reproduced with a few changes. First, the demand against supply model is renamed as a benefits against costs model. The demand curve has been renamed as MSB, which stands for marginal social benefits and is the benefits associated with one more unit of output. This doesn't change the analysis as a marginal social benefits curve is a demand curve if consumers are the only ones to benefit from the product or service, which they most likely will be. The (total) supply curve from the last diagram has been renamed as MSC, which stands for marginal social costs and is the costs associated with one more unit of output. This also doesn't change the analysis, as the (upward sloping part of a) marginal cost curve is the same thing as a supply curve.

The second change to the diagram shown earlier is that two other marginal costs/supply curves have been added alongside the MSC curve, which now represent the constituent parts of the MSC curve. These are the MPC curve, or marginal private costs, and the MEC curve, or marginal external costs. In the earlier diagram demand or MSC = MPC, and the only relevant costs making up the marginal social costs were those to the private supplier/producer/seller (MPC). But now with externalities present MSC = MPC + MEC, as both private costs (MPC) and unintended external costs (MEC) are present and play a role.

Private & social incentives differ

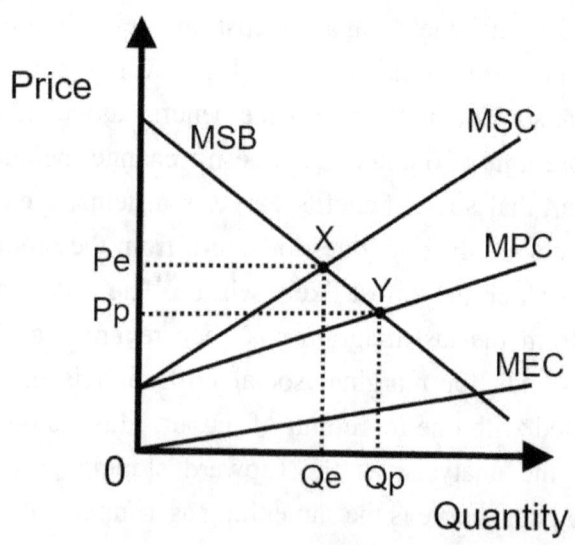

Just as in the first diagram in this section point X represents the efficient equilibrium point where all needs and sides are in perfect balance. Where (total) supply = demand, and marginal (total social) costs MSC = marginal social benefits MSB, with equilibrium price at Pe and equilibrium quantity of output supplied/demanded at Qe. But the existence of pollution externalities changes the expected long-run stable outcome which will actually occur to point Y, where private supply = demand, and marginal private costs MPC = marginal social benefits (MSB), with the price of the pollution causing activity at price Pp and the quantity of output supplied/demanded at Qp. As the diagram suggests, this outcome is inefficient and sees too much of the pollution causing activity when compared to the ideal equilibrium (as Qp > Qe), and the pollution causing activity is also at too low a price (as Pp < Pe). In other words there is a market failure to reach the best outcome.

Pollution externalities don't change the fact that the expected long-run outcome occurs where a private producer or private seller's supply equals a consumer or buyer's demand. The change in outcome which sees too much pollution at too low a price is due to pollution externalities raising the total social costs and therefore supply of an activity or product, from just private costs (MSC = MPC) to both private costs and the costs of the pollution externalities (MSC = MPC + MEC).

In changing the costs pollution externalities also change the incentives, from a situation where total social incentives = private incentives, to a situation where social incentives = private incentives + unintended externalities. This simple equation highlights the problem when pollution externalities are present, which is that social incentives are not equal to private incentives. In simple terms the problem is that a private producer or seller doesn't have the incentive to take responsibility for all of the costs their products will inflict upon society, only those costs borne directly (private costs) and not those they can offload onto others (external costs). Naturally this lack of responsibility creates a situation where pollution and environmental degradation are at excessive levels, as we can see in the real world today.

The challenge and the solution to the market failure which causes excess pollution and environmental degradation is to realign social and private incentives, to reach the efficient equilibrium where the total supply and social costs of an activity are matched with the total demand for and the social benefits of that activity. And this is done by making the polluter responsible for all of the MEC and pollution externalities that they cause, which is sometimes known as the 'Polluter Pays Principle'. In order for this to happen a polluter must be made to internalise all of the external costs of their pollution causing activity.

At the ideal and efficient equilibrium the marginal external costs (MEC) of a pollution causing activity will equal the marginal abatement costs (MAC) of the activity, MEC = MAC. While external costs represent the supply of pollution as just explained, and the cost of one more unit of pollution, abatement costs represent a polluter's demand for pollution, and the cost of reducing one more unit of pollution (e.g. the sacrificed output which goes hand in hand with pollution). The higher the MEC value the higher the supply of pollution, and the higher the MAC value the higher the polluter's demand for pollution (due to a higher cost of reducing it). So the solution to the environmental externalities problems, MAC = MEC, is to make a polluter's pollution demand = pollution supply, to see the benefits and costs of pollution in balance. This is achieved by making the polluter pay for the costs of their pollution, which should have the effect of causing a polluter to act on and reveal their marginal abatement costs and pollution demand, bringing about an efficient equilibrium outcome. There are various methods which may be used to make a polluter pay for their pollution, and these are put forward over the next several sections, beginning with the concept of bargaining.

3 Pollution Control Instruments

3.1 Bargaining and the Coase Theorem

One possible solution to the pollution problem is for the different sides to come together, polluter and the victims of pollution, and attempt to bring about an agreement where one side hands over money in an attempt to make things right. However, this idea does not involve the polluter paying the victims of pollution money as compensation for the costs they've had to endure. Although it may seem fair that a victim of pollution should be paid by those responsible for it, in practice this would create the wrong incentives. Victims of pollution could simply agree to tolerate high levels of pollution in order to receive the financial compensation, and the poorest and most desperate people may even encourage and facilitate greater pollution in their area in an attempt to acquire a financial payout. This could counteract the reduced incentive to create pollution which the compensation requirement puts upon a polluter, and therefore the whole idea of a polluter paying the victims of pollution directly isn't likely to create an efficient equilibrium outcome.

But the opposite scenario where a victim pays a polluter a 'bribe' in an attempt to discourage pollution may work. This idea sounds ridiculous for two reasons, the first being that it is clearly unfair for a victim to have to pay a perpetrator to stop harming them, and the second reason being that the idea seems to represent the exact opposite of the 'Polluter Pays Principle' thought to resolve the incentive to pollute. Yet the practice of the victims of pollution paying the polluter to reduce pollution can be effective. It has a clear advantage over the opposite scenario where a polluter compensates the victims in that it encourages a supposed victim to accurately report the costs of pollution, as a victim gains nothing by exaggerating them as they are only increasing their own payment costs. And despite the appearance to the contrary, the efficient Polluter Pays Principle is actually at work indirectly when victims must bribe polluters to stop. The more a polluter continues to pollute under such a system the larger the payoff bribe they will miss out on from a pollution victim, and although a polluter may not pay directly with higher costs, they therefore will pay indirectly with lost revenue.

The situation where the victims of pollution attempt to incentivize polluters to reduce their environmental degradation is known as bargaining. And although a range of outcomes are possible in this negotiation, from the polluter not reducing their pollution at all, to eliminating it completely, and everywhere in between, in theory bargaining can help achieve the efficient outcome where the benefits and the costs of pollution are equally matched.

In the last section the efficient equilibrium outcome was revealed to occur where the marginal external costs of polluting output (MEC), or pollution supply, are equal to the polluter's marginal abatement costs of pollution (MAC), which is their demand for pollution, MEC = MAC. And this efficient outcome can be written in another way which is more relevant to the bargaining model, by saying that MEC = MPB. MPB refers to the marginal private benefits the polluter receives from polluting output, and MEC the costs incurred upon the pollution victims. This replacement of marginal abatement costs (MAC) with marginal private benefits (MPB) doesn't change the principle, and marginal abatement costs, the cost of reducing one more unit of pollution, is essentially the same as marginal private benefits, the benefits associated with one more unit of polluting output. A lower MAC and a lower MPB both mean a producer will be more willing to reduce their level of polluting output, while a higher MAC and a higher MPB both mean a producer will be less willing to reduce their level of polluting output.

The following diagram may show how bargaining can work more clearly. The horizontal axis again shows the quantity (Q) of the pollution causing activity, as in the last diagram. And the vertical axis again shows the price of the pollution causing activity, which is simplified to the monetary value here ($). The upward sloping MEC line shows the marginal external costs of pollution a consumer faces, while the downward sloping MPB represents the marginal private benefits (i.e. profits) of pollution for the polluting producer. All of the other information in the graph, the marked levels of Q, and the labelled triangles from a to d, are there to show the factors motivating the bargaining process between polluter and pollution victim.

If the polluter was left to their own devices, without any interference or payoffs from outside parties, they would naturally produce a quantity (Q) of their pollution causing activity which maximized their returns and profits. And the returns and benefits for a producer would only be maximized when every last possible penny had been generated from the pollution causing activity, and the marginal benefits had fallen to zero. This occurs in the diagram at point Q2, where the marginal private benefits (MPB) curve cuts the horizontal axis. Therefore a pollution causing producer may be expected to prefer to produce at a Q2 quantity of output. This is based on the simplifying assumption that a producer's marginal private costs are zero, as a producer of course wouldn't select an output level where marginal costs were greater than marginal benefits, as that would see the producer incur a loss. However, the producer's choice of a Q2 level of output is inefficient, and as the diagram reveals at this point the marginal external monetary costs ($ MEC) of the pollution causing activity are significantly higher than the marginal private monetary benefits ($ MPB). But as a pollution victim suffers far more from the Q2 output level than the producer gains, the bargaining process could potentially resolve this problem.

Bargaining welfare effects

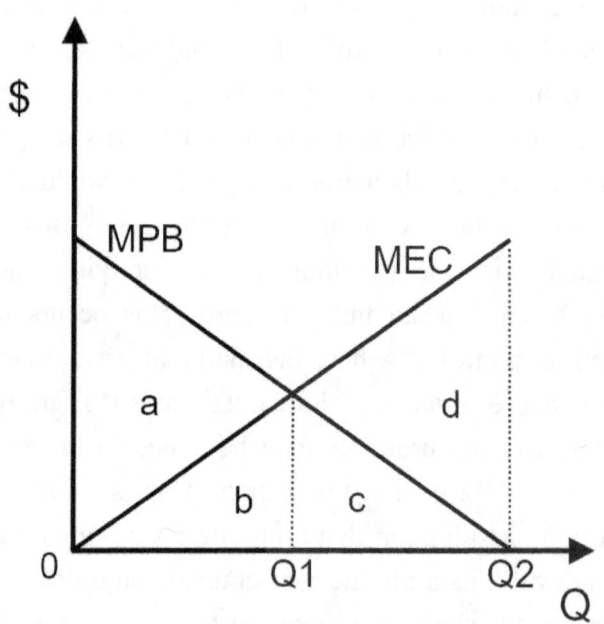

A pollution victim may decide to offer a payoff bribe to the polluting producer, to give an incentive for the producer to select a lower level of output. If the producer was to select an output level of quantity Q1 instead of quantity Q2, for example, then the producer would miss out on MPB gains of the size given by triangle 'c' (i.e. everything under the MPB line, between output quantity levels Q1 and Q2). But a polluting producer output level of Q1 instead of Q2 would reduce a consumer's suffering to a far greater extent, and a consumer would reduce their MEC losses by the amount given by triangle 'c' plus triangle 'd' (i.e. everything under the MEC line, between Q1 and Q2). And therefore a consumer victim of pollution could offer a payoff greater than 'c' but less than 'c' plus 'd', to persuade a producer to select the less harmful output level quantity Q1 in place of the higher output quantity Q2. This outcome is better for the consumer victim, as Q2 output MEC losses of 'c' plus 'd' are replaced with a payoff bribe cost loss lower than 'c' plus 'd'. And it's also better and therefore acceptable for a producer, as Q2 output pollution profit gains of size 'c' are replaced by payoff income from the consumer which exceeds 'c'. And the Q1 producer output level is also the efficient outcome, as while at Q2 the costs of pollution (MEC) exceed the benefits it generates (MPB), with output level Q1 both the costs and benefits of pollution are balanced as MEC = MPB and the two lines cross.

In an ideal world the consumer who suffers from pollution would like the polluting producer to select an output quantity even lower than level Q1. But this desire is likely to go unmet as a producer output level below quantity Q1 is inefficient, as it sees the benefits of pollution (MPB) outweigh the costs (MEC). While this may sound like a desirable scenario there is no way for it to be achieved with a bargaining situation, and bargaining can't reduce the output level of the polluting producer any lower than level Q1. This is because the potential payoff bribe a consumer would be willing to offer simply won't be enough to incentivise a polluting producer to willingly sacrifice the monetary benefits associated with pollution.

For example, if a producer was to select an output level of 0 in the previous diagram, instead of output level Q1, then they would miss out on MPB gains of the size of triangles 'a' plus 'b' (i.e. everything under the MPB line, between output quantity levels 0 and Q1). But the reduction in output from Q1 to 0 would only reduce a consumer victim of pollution's MEC losses to the amount given by triangle 'b' (i.e. everything under the MEC line, between 0 and Q1). To be willing to give up output production from Q1 to 0 a polluting producer would expect to be compensated by a monetary amount greater than 'a' plus 'b'. Yet a consumer could only offer a payoff which was less than 'b' or they would be better off just accepting the higher output and pollution by the producer.

The Coase Theorem

The Coase Theorem formally notes the potential which bargaining has to bring about a superior efficient outcome when externalities are present. The theorem states that irrespective of the original allocation of property rights bargaining will result in a Pareto efficient outcome, where no individual can be made better off without making another individual worse off, under the assumptions that trade in the externality is possible and transaction costs are sufficiently low. This is an important result as it reveals the potential for people to resolve the problem of externalities themselves, without a need for government intervention or litigation which may bring their own problems.

However, in practice bargaining has its limitations. In many cases property rights are not well defined, and therefore it may be difficult for a bargaining situation to arise. For example, if a producer was polluting a local water supply with toxic materials then a bargaining situation may be set up with the local residents whose water supply was affected. But if a producer was polluting the air with large quantities of non-toxic greenhouse gas emissions such as methane or carbon dioxide then the question of who exactly to set up a bargaining exchange with is uncertain. Greenhouse gas emission damage may only occur in the distant future through climate change, the results of which are often unpredictable, and it may affect people on the other side of the world who can't be identified.

Coase himself acknowledged that while bargaining may work in theory in practice significant transaction costs often stand in the way. For example, a victim of pollution may not know the precise source of their suffering, and they may lack the time and resources to find this out to begin a bargaining process. Alternatively, a polluting producer may not know the monetary value of the benefits of pollution, or a consumer victim may not know the monetary costs of pollution upon themselves, and either party may lack the time or resources to discover this information to bring about an efficient bargaining outcome. Finally, if there are many bargainers in a bargaining situation there may be disagreement upon the value of externalities, and this can also prevent an efficient outcome from being reached.

In summary bargaining may bring about an efficient outcome where the benefits and costs of pollution externalities are equal and balanced, but in practice this is unlikely in most situations as it depends upon a small number of bargainers, low transaction costs, and well informed participants. And if these conditions are not met then there may be a need for outside intervention to deal with externalities. This is examined in the next section.

3.2 Command and Control Policy

The last section noted that the problem of environmental externalities causing an inefficient outcome might not be resolved with bargaining between the affected parties. And therefore government intervention may be required to bring about a better outcome. One common type of government intervention into the issue of environmental externalities is a command and control policy, which sees a government issue a range of quantitative (quantity) or qualitative (quality) commands and controls to prevent a producer from creating excess pollution externalities.

For example, a quantitative control measure could put limits upon the permissible levels of greenhouse gas emissions for a producer. And a qualitative command measure could impose a minimum standard of technology, thought to be less harmful than an older or lesser standard of technology. Or a qualitative control measure may see government restrict polluting producers from areas with large numbers of people, or important environmental features, in an attempt to limit the damage pollution can cause. And if a polluting producer doesn't follow the commands and controls they face significant fines from government, which enforces the polluter's pay principle.

Command and control policy has an essential role to play in pollution control, and in cases where zero pollution is acceptable, such as with highly dangerous and toxic pollutants, it is the most effective and perhaps only viable method to use. However, in practice most pollutants being released into the atmosphere today are not highly dangerous and toxic, and while most pollutants do cause some damage to the environment they are often an inseparable part of productive output. And therefore, despite its popularity with some governments, a command and control regulation policy is highly unlikely to be efficient or bring about an efficient outcome where the benefits and costs of pollution are balanced and equal. It was noted earlier that an efficient outcome will occur where a producer's marginal abatement costs (MAC) for pollution equal the marginal external costs (MEC) of pollution, but government command and control regulation imposes a set standard on all pollution and ignores the difference in marginal abatement costs which polluting producers will have. And this by definition ensures that pollution MAC will not always equal pollution MEC when command and control regulation is used.

In order for a pollution abatement policy to be feasible cost efficiency is a very important feature, and this condition requires that pollution abatement occurs at the minimum possible cost. In practice this would require that those polluting producers with the lowest marginal costs of abatement undertake most of the abatement, and those with the highest marginal costs of abatement undertake the least (but still some), in order to equalize the marginal costs of abatement at the minimum possible value across all polluting producers. This is a pollution externality example of the equimarginal principle, which states that the efficient equilibrium outcome will occur where marginal values are all equalized. However, with a command and control policy only concerning itself with the levels of pollution being caused by producers, and never accounting for their differing relative circumstances and marginal costs to ensure that lower cost abaters abate more, the equimarginal principle is not followed and cost efficiency is missed.

A command and control policy can also be a highly cost inefficient method to monitor and enforce. While it is easy for a government to make rules for polluting firms, it can cost a large amount of money to make sure the rules are followed. Constant investing in modern technology and hiring workers to monitor pollution levels can be expensive, and having to enforce the rules with proper punishments is also likely to increase the cost inefficiency of a command and control policy.

With command and control measures clearly having their limitations an alternative method of government intervention may be required to deal with externality issues. The next section addresses this by looking into the popular concept of Pigovian taxation.

3.3 Pigovian Taxation

It has been noted that an efficient equilibrium exists where the marginal benefits of pollution equal the marginal costs of pollution. One method used to achieve this goal is to set a tax on the polluters at the source of the externalities, in an attempt to raise their marginal costs. This idea is known as a Pigovian tax after the creator Arthur Cecil Pigou. To see the difference this makes the following diagram first offers a reminder of the market failure outcome caused by pollution externalities, before a Pigovian tax is set.

Before Pigovian taxation

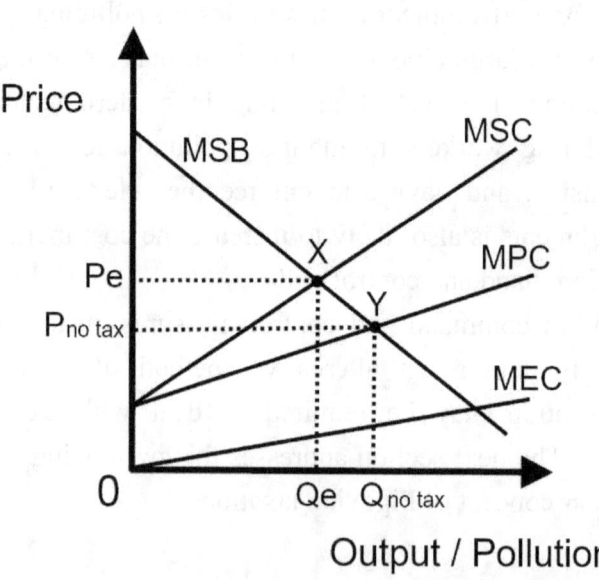

As noted earlier, the original outcome (before any solutions such as Pigovian taxation are attempted) caused by pollution externalities sees a disparity between social incentives and private incentives, and a resulting inefficient outcome. Pollution externalities (marginal external costs, MEC) have created a situation where the total social costs of output (marginal social costs, MSC) are no longer equal to the polluting producer's costs (marginal private costs, MPC), but have risen to the level of MSC = MPC + MEC. Yet a private polluting producer has no incentive to take account for these MEC pollution externalities, and will instead make its choice of output (and therefore pollution) at the profit-maximizing point where marginal benefits equal its private marginal costs.

Marginal benefits for the producer here are given by MSB, marginal social benefits, as with no externality benefits (only costs) to the polluter's output the marginal social benefits are exactly the same as marginal private (producer) benefits, MPB = MSB, and the two terms can be used interchangeably. And the marginal costs for the producer are given by MPC, marginal private costs. The diagram shows that the profit-maximizing point where a producer's marginal benefits and marginal costs are equal, MSB = MPC, occurs at point Y. And therefore without outside intervention the outcome will be point Y, with output at quantity level Q $_{no\ tax}$, and at price P $_{no\ tax}$. And as the diagram shows this sees output and pollution at too low a price relative to the efficient equilibrium price Pe, and at too high a quantity level relative to equilibrium output quantity Qe, where MSB = MSC at point X and all externalities are accounted for.

The goal of Pigovian taxation is to change the incentives facing a polluting producer, in an attempt to reach the efficient equilibrium outcome at point X with efficient price and quantity levels for output and pollution. By levying a tax (t) on a polluting producer government aims to change their marginal cost curve from MPC to MPC + t, so that a polluter has to account for externalities.

With Pigovian taxation

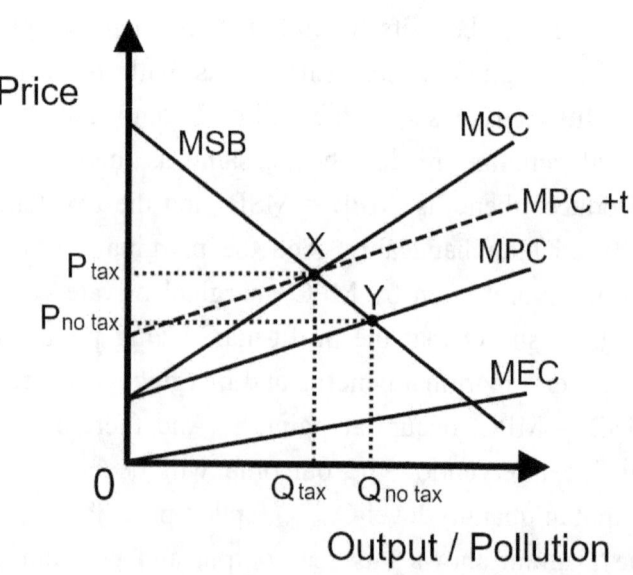

The idea is that a polluter producer will no longer be able to able to select its profit-maximizing point at inefficient point Y, where MSB = MPC, as the MPC line will have been completely removed by government and replaced with the pricier MPC + t line, where a tax is added to marginal costs. And therefore the producer will have no choice but to select its profit-maximizing point where MSB = MPC + t. And if the tax has been set at the correct rate as in the diagram this should occur at the same point where MSB = MSC, ensuring the producer selects optimum efficient equilibrium point X, with price P_{tax} the equilibrium price, and output quantity Q_{tax} the equilibrium output level. At this optimum equilibrium point X the tax t = MEC (note that this diagram has not been drawn to scale), and as the marginal abatement cost MAC = MEC at the equilibrium, it is also true that tax t = MAC at this optimum.

While this section has focused upon environmental taxes, government could use subsidies instead and the same efficient equilibrium outcome should still be achieved. Just as an environmental tax will cause a polluter to abate pollution so long as the marginal abatement cost is lower than the unit cost of the tax, an environmental subsidy will cause a polluter to abate only if the unit abatement subsidy exceeds the polluter's marginal abatement cost. The main difference is that a tax will reduce a polluter's income, while a subsidy will increase it. And in the long-run, with large amounts of lump sum subsidies paid to polluting polluters, there is a risk that a Pigovian subsidy policy could change the profitability of polluters, and the size of the industry. And this could end the equivalence of subsidy and tax policies, as subsidies may no longer be associated with an equilibrium efficient outcome. This combined with the sheer cost to government of a subsidy scheme suggest that Pigovian taxes are preferable to subsidies.

There are several benefits associated with the use of a Pigovian tax. First, unlike some other government measures used to deal with pollution externalities (e.g. command and control instruments) a Pigovian tax is a market system and is therefore cost efficient. Those polluting producers with the lowest abatement costs (i.e. the lowest cost to reduce pollution) will abate and reduce their polluting output most to pay a lower tax bill, as it costs the producers less to abate than to pay tax for not abating. And the polluting producers with the highest abatement costs (i.e. the highest cost to reduce pollution) will abate and reduce their polluting output the least and pay a higher tax bill, as it costs the producers more to abate than to pay tax for not abating. Second, as well as being cost efficient and making the best use of available resources, known as static efficiency, a Pigovian tax also encourages innovation in pollution reduction technologies by producers in order to reduce costs, and is therefore also dynamically efficient. Third, environmental taxes such as Pigovian taxes generate revenue for government, which can then be spent on various beneficial programs or policies. There is some evidence that Pigovian taxes can generate a so-called 'double dividend' and two different benefits, and that as well as reducing environmental pollution (the first dividend), the taxes can generate revenue in place of other taxes which have damaging effects upon economic growth, thereby increasing a country's macroeconomic performance (the second dividend). Finally, the cost of monitoring and enforcing a Pigovian tax is likely to be lower than with a command and control policy. With the latter monitoring and enforcement is the only thing keeping the system from falling apart, but with a market-based Pigovian tax the system can run itself.

However, there are also some drawbacks associated with Pigovian taxation. The most obvious one is that they may not be equitable. The costs of environmental taxes set on polluting firms are likely to be passed on to consumers, and this may mean higher heating and fuel costs for all, which has the potential to drive the poorest people below the poverty line. This issue could be resolved if a redistributive tax policy was used alongside the Pigovian taxation, but such a redistributive tax policy is likely to be inefficient and therefore may take away some of the efficiency benefits associated with Pigovian taxation.

Another possible drawback with Pigovian taxation is linked with the difficulty and cost associated with determining the efficient rate for the environmental tax. And this could suggest that Pigovian taxes won't perform quite as well in practice as they do in theory. First, it can be very difficult to determine the actual costs of pollution, as it may have not only environmental and economic effects, but also psychological effects which are specific to each individual. And if different types of pollution or pollution sources affect people differently then there would need to be many different Pigovian tax rates in order to ensure efficiency. But performing the extensive research required to determine all of these tax rates may be very expensive or not even feasible.

Second, powerful political lobbying groups may lead a government to believe that pollution externalities and costs are higher or lower than they are in reality, and then set an inefficient Pigovian tax level. Large corporations known for high pollution levels may lobby government with distorted evidence that pollution is less harmful than it really is, resulting in a too low a tax level, or environmental organizations may lobby and convince government that pollution is more harmful than it really is, causing too low a tax rate. Alternatively lobby groups with no interest in environmental issues may simply distract government's focus elsewhere, and cause a Pigovian tax rate which is either too high or low.

Third, Pigovian taxes ignore the reciprocal nature of pollution externalities, and while they may address the issue of polluting firms pushing external costs onto consumers, they ignore the fact that consumers themselves can increase the impact of these external costs. For example, a polluting firm may at first only be guilty of polluting fifty people who live in a polluted area, and pay a Pigovian tax which corresponds to this marginal external cost. But if another fifty people moved into the polluted area then the marginal external cost of the producer's pollution would rise, despite no change in the polluter's behaviour or level of emissions, as more people would suffer the effects of pollution. And the theory of Pigovian taxation would suggest that the polluter should then pay more in tax, creating a situation where a polluter is punished for things it can't control. This theoretical example suggests that setting Pigovian taxes may be more complicated than first thought.

Bearing in mind the potential problems associated with Pigovian taxes the next section looks into an alternative way of dealing with pollution externalities, using tradable emissions permits.

3.4 Tradable Emissions Permits

Tradable emissions permits, also known as transferable or marketable emissions permits, differ from Pigovian taxes in that instead of using prices and costs they work with quantities. But tradable emissions permits (TEP) differ from command and control instruments, which also work in terms of quantities, in that they allow for the quantities of permissible pollution emissions to be transferred. TEP essentially create a market for pollution for the right to pollute, the intention being that those polluting producers who gain the most from pollution or have the highest abatement costs will pay money to buy more emission permits, while those polluting producers who gain the least from pollution or have the lowest abatement costs will sell their own emissions permits for money. TEP offer the same market incentives as Pigovian taxes in this respect, in that they are designed to motivate the polluters with the lowest abatement costs to abate pollution the most, and those with the highest abatement costs to abate least, creating an efficient equilibrium outcome.

A tradable emissions permit (TEP) scheme requires a government to go through several steps:

1) First a government will decide on its targeted level of pollution, and as a result the number of pollution permits it will issue, in units of pollution;

2) Next a government will decide on how to allocate pollution permits. For example it might decide to auction them out, so that those who value polluting more and have higher abatement costs purchase the most permits right from the start in an attempt to encourage efficiency. Or government might follow its own rule of thumb and make allowances for differing circumstances, such as basing permit allocation on likely pollution needs with larger firms given more permits than smaller firms;

3) Once the original allocation of TEPs has been made a government will then create a system which guarantees the free trade of permits. Those polluters who wish to pollute more than their permits allow must be free and able to buy permits for additional units of pollution, while those polluters who wish to pollute less than their permits allow must be able to sell their permits for units of pollution for money;

4) With pollution permits allocated, and free trade in permits ensured, government must then make sure that each polluter follows the rules and their level of pollution does not exceed the level which their permits entitle them to. This step involves three separate components. One, government must state and make it clear that a polluter is prohibited from releasing an amount of pollution emissions beyond the number of permits they hold. Well-publicized and official government correspondence could help with this goal. Two, government must monitor the

actual emissions levels of all polluters. This should be a relatively simple task, although potentially expensive, using modern technology. Third and finally, government must enforce the rule that no-one can emit more than their permits allow. And this means that anyone who breaks this rule is punished for it, perhaps with heavy fines far beyond the pollution cost, or alternatively through government putting operating restrictions on a polluter for a period.

Once a government has proceeded through the above four steps an efficient transferable emissions permit scheme should come about naturally as follows:

a) Polluting firms compare the price of emissions permits with their own individual marginal abatement costs;

b) Each polluting firm decides how much it will pollute;

c) Firms trade permits between each other, based on their decision to either abate pollution, or hold permits and have the right to pollute. Firms with higher abatement costs will be the ones buying more permits to pollute, as this costs them less than abating pollution. And firms with lower abatement costs will be the ones selling permits, as abating pollution costs them less than the price of permits.

Just like Pigovian taxes TEPs should achieve the efficient equilibrium outcome at the lowest cost to ensure cost efficiency. And as a consequence the marginal abatement costs of all polluting firms will be equal at the equilibrium point, as the equimarginal principle predicts. The end result is a market for pollution where a single equilibrium price for pollution permits emerges, where the cost of a permit reflects the true cost of pollution (the marginal external cost, MEC). At the equilibrium the price of a permit = MEC = MAC.

A simple numerical example can help show how transferable emissions permit work in practice. Suppose that there are two polluting firms, firm A and firm B. The cost of reducing pollution by one ton at firm A's power plant (i.e. firm A's marginal cost of abatement, MAC) is £30. And the cost of reducing pollution by one ton at firm B's power plant (i.e. firm B's MAC) is £50. Government tells both firm A and firm B that their pollution levels are too high, and that each firm must lower their pollution levels by 10 tons, for a total pollution reduction of 20 tons. Without the government issuing TEPs this would cost firm A £300 (as firm A's MAC is £30 per ton, and a 10 ton abatement requirement gives £30*10 = £300), and it would cost firm B £500 (as firm B's MAC is £50 per ton, and a 10 ton abatement requirement gives £50*10 = £500). The total social cost of the pollution abatement to the level required by government would therefore be £300 + £500 = £800, if transferable emissions permits are not used (i.e. if government just tells polluters what they have to do, with a command and control policy).

However, if TEPs are introduced the result changes completely. Suppose that government decides to issue each of the two polluting firms in this example, firm A and firm B, with 10 transferable emissions permits each for a total permit allowance of 10 tons of pollution each (i.e. 1 permit allows 1 ton of pollution). Firm A could reduce its own pollution levels by 20 tons and complete all of the pollution reduction required by government all by itself, and sell its tradable permit allowances to firm B so that firm B can get away with not reducing its own pollution emissions at all. And because firm A has a lower marginal cost of abatement than firm B the total social cost of the pollution reduction would be far lower, at only £600 (as firm A's MAC is £30 per ton of pollution, and a 20 ton reduction gives £30*20 = £600) instead of the £800 it would cost if permits weren't used. Firm A and firm B would both be willing to go along with this trade as long as it meant lower costs.

Without trade in TEPs firm A's 10 ton required pollution reduction would cost £300 as just earlier, and therefore in order to go ahead with the trade it would want to end up with a cost lower than £300 after both a 20 ton pollution reduction and selling its 10 pollution permits to firm B for money. We already know that the 20 ton pollution reduction (i.e. firm A meeting the pollution requirements of both firms) costs firm A £600, and therefore firm A's sale of its 10 permits to firm B must be for more than £300 (i.e. at least £300.01). To prove this the £600 cost of pollution reduction can be denoted as –600, and the (minimum required) income from the sale of permits to firm B can be denoted as +300.01, and the sum of the two gives 300.01 – 600 = –299.99 or a £299.99 cost. As this is a lower cost than the £300 firm A would have to pay if there was no trade in pollution permits, firm A would happily make the trade.

Without trade in TEPs firm B's 10 ton required pollution reduction would cost £500 as explained earlier, and therefore in order to go ahead with the trade firm B would want to end up with a cost lower than £500 after buying 10 permits from firm A. Putting firm B's requirement for trade in TEPs to go ahead, that 10 permits < £500, with firm A's requirement for trade in TEPs to go ahead, that 10 permits > £300, gives the following overall result: £300 < 10 TEPs < £500, or in other words 10 permits will cost more than £300 but less than £500.

This result reveals two pieces of information. First, as the individual requirements for firm A and firm B don't clash with each other we know that the trade will go ahead, and TEPs are a feasible way to reach an efficient equilibrium outcome. Second, we know that the equilibrium price of 1 tradable emissions permit in this example, and the shadow or estimated price of pollution will be (found by dividing by ten): £30 < 1 TEP < £50. The equilibrium price of one TEP will be between £30 and

£50 in this example. The precise value will likely depend on the power dynamics between the two producers. If firm B was in desperate need for more emissions permits and didn't have the time to negotiate the price may be closer to £50, the most they'd be willing to pay, as firm B decides to avoid a drawn out bargaining process with firm A and pays a higher price. But if firm B planned ahead and didn't need the permits urgently, yet firm A was in desperate need for money, then the price of one TEP may be closer to £30, the least firm A would accept, as firm A decides to avoid a drawn out bargaining process.

Note that while in this example both firms were allocated the same amount of permits, and given the same pollution reduction target by government, TEPs can create a more efficient outcome even if this is not the case. The abatement undertaken and the equilibrium price does not depend on the initial allocation of permits, but only on the quantity of permits issued. Irrespective of the initial allocation of permits, or the allocation of pollution reduction targets, the firms with lower marginal abatement costs will choose to sell their permits to those with higher marginal abatement costs for profit, while those firms with higher MACs will choose to buy permits from those with lower MACs to lower their own costs.

As tradable emissions permits (TEPs) can bring about an efficient equilibrium outcome just as Pigovian taxes can bring about an efficient equilibrium outcome, it follows that the two different types of pollution control methods should result in the same price or cost for polluters. And if the total number of TEPs issued by government (i.e. the acceptable and equilibrium level of pollution decided by government) is the same as the level of pollution which exists after Pigovian taxes have been set (i.e. the acceptable and equilibrium pollution level decided by government), as it should be, then the equilibrium market price of a permit will equal the optimal environmental tax rate. This is an intuitive result, as paying an environmental tax directly to government is essentially the same thing as paying indirectly for a government issued and controlled tradable emissions permit.

But while TEPs and Pigovian taxes both offer the same incentives to polluters, there may be differences between them in the long-run depending on how the TEPs are initially distributed. If the TEP system is truly competitive, and permits are distributed freely by government at the outset, then TEP and environmental tax schemes should have the same efficient result. But if the TEPs were auctioned off by the government to polluters at a price at the outset then there will be a net transfer from polluters to government, and this could have negative consequences in the long-run by causing income distribution issues. A government run auction process is a net transfer of income from polluting firms to government and is essentially an unnecessary tax on firms, which is therefore likely to cause long-run inefficiency in the firms' industry.

Overall tradable emissions permits can bring about an efficient equilibrium outcome and achieve a specific pollution target, without the difficulties in having to determine the specifics of the system seen with a Pigovian tax policy. And while a TEP system may come with monitoring and enforcement costs these costs are likely to be far lower than those of a command and control policy, as the latter is based entirely on government monitoring and enforcement while a TEP system relies on firms trading with each other in a free market, with monitoring and enforcement only an accompaniment to this.

But despite its strengths there are many pitfalls inherent in a TEP system. First, the allocation of permits may cause income distribution issues between firms and government if they are auctioned off, as just noted. Second, an efficient permit trading system can only exist if firms are aware of other firms' possession of permits, and their willingness to trade them. And this may require a degree of cooperation and level of information sharing which firms won't agree to. Third, any system which encourages firms to share information on their possession and willingness to trade permits may create a strategic 'us vs them' mentality, as firms considered one of 'us' trade information and permits with each other for profit gains, while rival competitors or new firms are kept out of the loop and denied information or permit trades to keep them inefficient and reduce industry competition. In other words an efficient TEP system depends on the free trade of permits, but the information requirement may prevent truly free trade. Fourth, if firms are allowed to bank permits for long periods and hold on to them despite not having immediate plans to use them, then there is a risk that baseless speculation could limit the trade of permits and ruin the efficiency of the TEP system. For example, a firm may not have any need for permits but hold onto them instead of selling them, as it (incorrectly) thinks the permits can be sold for a higher price than the going rate, or (incorrectly) believes that the selling price of permits may rise in the future due to various external factors. Finally, many argue that a TEP system is immoral, as it may result in either rich Western firms simply buying all the pollution permits held by firms in poorer countries to avoid having to abate pollution themselves, or less efficient firms in poorer countries having to spend their limited resources buying permits from more efficient firms in richer Western countries to lower costs. To avoid these power dynamics it is therefore often suggested that permit trading schemes are kept as internal systems within a country only, or within regions which have already free trade such as the European Union.

3.5 Pollution Control Analysis

The last four sections on Bargaining, Command and Control, Pigovian Taxation, and Tradable Emissions Permits have examined four different methods to control and reduce pollution levels. Each pollution control method has been found to come with its own different advantages and disadvantages, but the bargaining method was noted as only being likely to be useful when dealing with a small number of bargainers (e.g. one polluter and a small number of local victims of pollution), and an efficient bargaining system may break down when this isn't the case. Because of this a bargaining method is unlikely to be a realistic solution to the global problem of mass pollution, and therefore it will be left out from the analysis and comparison in this section which attempts to find out which of the pollution control methods is the best. The rest of this section therefore examines Command and Control Policy, Pigovian Taxation, and Tradable Emissions Permits, bringing all of the information from the past three sections together with additional analysis to compare how the various methods fare in terms of several important criteria: cost efficiency (also known as static efficiency), dynamic efficiency, equity and income distribution effects, and performance under uncertainty.

Cost efficiency (static efficiency)

In order for a command and control method to be cost efficient government must meet two criteria: 1) government must know a polluter's cost of abatement function, which is the relationship between a firm's output/pollution levels and its marginal cost of abatement; 2) government must calculate an optimal pollution emission target for each individual firm, based on the principle that those firms with the lowest costs of abatement abate the most, and those firms with the highest costs of abatement abate the least. These two tasks are likely to be very difficult to achieve, and therefore it is unlikely that a command and control policy will be cost efficient in achieving a pollution target.

Market systems on the other hand, such as Pigovian taxation and tradable emissions permits, can achieve any pollution level at the lowest cost. Irrespective of the tax level set by government or the number of permits issued these market systems will create a situation where the lowest cost abaters abate the most pollution, to avoid the higher cost of Pigovian taxes or to make a profit selling permits for a higher amount. And these market systems will also see the highest cost abaters abate pollution the least, as abatement costs more than just paying an environmental tax for polluting or buying pollution permits. Therefore both Pigovian taxation and tradable emissions permits are far more cost efficient than command and control policy.

One other factor affecting the cost efficiency of a pollution control method is the cost of monitoring, administrating and enforcing the methods. And market instruments such as Pigovian taxation or tradable emissions permits are also likely to be more cost efficient than a command and control policy in this respect. With taxation or permits the government simply has to decide on the tax level or number of permits issued, and then the system runs itself through market incentives, with the government only having to ensure taxes are paid or that no-one pollutes without the required number of permits. But with a command and control policy there is no natural system running itself, and therefore the cost of monitoring, administrating, and enforcing is likely to be far higher.

There may be some situations where a command and control policy is more cost efficient in terms of monitoring, administration, and enforcement costs however. In lesser developed countries there may not be an established market system culture or set of institutions, and attempting to establish such a culture may be highly expensive and time-consuming. In this situation the cost of attempting to maintain a Pigovian tax or emissions permit market system may be prohibitive, and although still expensive a command and control policy may turn out to be the more cost efficient of the three methods.

Dynamic efficiency

Dynamic efficiency refers to the situation where efficiency increases over time, typically due to increased innovation. A dynamically efficient pollution control method will therefore encourage firms to invest in research for innovation, and the Pigovian taxation method does just that. Under the Pigovian tax system firms know that their current pollution level is directly correlated with the amount of money they must pay to government in tax, and therefore to reduce their pollution level is to reduce their tax bill. This motivates firms to innovate in order to create greener technologies which create the same level of output but come with lower pollution emissions.

A command and control pollution control instrument is not dynamically efficient. It does not encourage innovation but only mandates a certain level of pollution, as opposed to financially rewarding ever lower levels of pollution as a dynamically efficient system requires. A tradable emissions permit system is a partially dynamically efficient system, as a firm which lowers emissions would be able to save money by buying fewer permits or selling those permits it already has for a profit, thereby motivating innovation in theory. But a permit system may not encourage innovation and be dynamically efficient to the same extent as a Pigovian taxation system. While a tax system is based on prices and offers direct financial rewards from government (i.e. tax cuts) for lower pollution and direct financial punishments for higher emissions, a permit system is based on quantities and it therefore only offers financial incentives for innovation on an indirect basis. The firm which lowers emissions under a permit scheme will need to buy fewer permits, or can sell more permits, but the actual financial gain depends upon the price which is agreed with another firm, and this extra step and lack of a direct relationship between pollution and profit is likely to reduce the incentive for innovation.

Equity and income distribution effects

There are a number of equity and income distribution concerns linked with all of the major pollution control methods, and while pollution control offers a gain to society in terms of reduced emissions, it is typically also linked with a loss in terms of the reduced firm output associated with those emissions. As would be expected, those people who suffer most from pollution are likely to gain most from any pollution control method, while those people who suffer least from pollution or who gain the most from polluting firms' output (i.e. the firms themselves, and consumers who avoid the effects of pollution) will likely lose the most from pollution control. It is also true that any country which unilaterally implements a pollution control method, which is essentially an output control method as output and pollution often can't be separated, will lose out as it is basically undermining its own competitiveness and sacrificing income. Therefore it is important that all countries are involved with pollution control systems.

In terms of specific pollution control methods, Pigovian taxation is especially vulnerable to having a negative impact on the equity within society. So called green taxes tend to either be set on polluting firms, which raises their costs and forces them to push higher prices onto consumers, or are set directly on products such as petrol where the consumers are the polluters. Either way it may be consumers which suffer the brunt of the tax. And while the richest people in society may be able to pay the higher costs easily the tax could push the poorest people in society below the poverty line, reducing the equity in society. Even ignoring the impact a tax may have on consumers, it is also true that the richest firms will be able to pay the tax easily, but for those poorer and smaller firms the tax may mean the difference between cutting even and being unable to cover their costs, forcing them to leave their industry. Pigovian taxation could therefore have negative effects on industry competitiveness, and a less competitive industry is likely to be a less equitable one where powerful firms can do as they please.

Looking beyond the rich and poor, a Pigovian tax may have negative effects on other disadvantaged or more vulnerable groups in society too. A tax on heating fuel for example would have a larger impact on the elderly who use heating fuel most than on younger people. Earlier on the idea of Pigovian taxes generating a double dividend was put forward, as they may generate revenue which would allow government to reduce inefficient taxes elsewhere in the economy, thereby stimulating economic growth. But such a policy may also be bad for equity, as if government was to reduce taxes on workers (an area likely to cause inefficiencies, and therefore likely to be under consideration) they are essentially increasing taxes on the unemployed and underemployed in relative terms, which again could be bad for equity. Pigovian taxation is therefore likely to be bad for equity, and as mentioned earlier side payments to vulnerable groups most at risk of being negatively affected by the tax are often desirable to prevent this.

Tradable emissions permits may also be bad for equity. As noted earlier if the permits are auctioned off when they are first distributed, instead of being given out freely, then there will be a net transfer of income from firms to government and associated income distribution issues. In the long-run as payments mount up this could cause inefficiency in an industry, as smaller and poorer firms are forced out by costs and industry competition is reduced, which can also reduce equity. The way government spends the revenue from these permit auctions could also affect equity, especially if they use it as a replacement for inefficient (but equitable) taxes as noted above with Pigovian taxation. And any permit scheme applied to both developed and developing countries is also likely to be unequitable, as poorer developing countries will be punished more in relative terms in having to reduce a given level of pollution/output. Just as with Pigovian taxation the solution to this would be to offer side payments to developing countries involved in the permit scheme, or to only have tradable emissions permit systems between countries of a similar wealth and situation.

Analysis of tax and permit market systems have revealed that there is often a trade-off between efficiency and equity, and the most efficient pollution control methods tend to be bad for equity. And it is only direct government intervention (in the form of side payments) which can correct this and restore equity. Therefore a less efficient and more government intervention focused pollution control method such as a command and control policy may actually be the best in terms of equity.

Performance under uncertainty

The previous subsections have evaluated the performance of different pollution control methods in terms of efficiency and equity, but it has been implicitly assumed that all pollution control methods are able to work exactly as they are intended. In practice this may not be the case, and this subsection examines the performance of the methods in various conditions of uncertainty.

All three pollution control methods examined in this section, whether command and control, Pigovian taxation, or tradable emissions permits, require that the government knows the efficient (and perhaps also equitable) level of pollution, to then issue the correct commands and controls, the right number of permits, or to set the correct tax level. But even if the government doesn't hold this information and is forced to operate under uncertainty in setting targets, both the tax and permit systems can achieve any target at the lowest abatement cost, which a command and control policy cannot. And while both market systems have the edge over command and control if government lacks full information, the permit method is likely to be superior to both taxes and command and control methods when it comes to flexibility and allowing the government to deal with changing information on optimal targets. This is because it is easier to change the number of permits issued (by issuing more, or buying back those already issued), than to go through the process of changing the level of a tax or commands and controls. However, if the new information the government received related to a certain type of pollution being far more dangerous than previously thought then a command and control pollution regulation would fare best, as the most direct method.

In the scenario where it is not government but firms which lack full information, for example if firms don't know their own pollution abatement costs, then the performance of the different pollution control methods can change dramatically. Without knowing their own abatement costs a firm can't know their optimal response to a pollution tax (i.e. low abatement cost firms should abate but high abatement cost firms are better off not abating and just paying the tax), and this can create a situation where abatement doesn't occur at the lowest cost, and the level of abatement is unknown and not optimal. And without knowing their own abatement costs a firm can't know their optimal policy in a tradable permit system (i.e. low abatement cost firms should abate and sell their pollution permits to others, but high abatement cost firms are better off not abating and just buying pollution permits), which can create a situation where permits aren't bought from those who need them least by those who need them most, and therefore the price of permits and the price of pollution is unknown and not optimal. When firms face uncertainty the two market pollution control methods, taxes and permits, may not give the same result, and neither method can be relied upon to be more efficient than command and control regulation. In situations of uncertainty the best pollution control method is uncertain.

4 Efficient Environmental Management

4.1 Renewable Natural Resources

All of the discussion so far has focused on pollution, and how best to balance the benefits and costs of pollution causing output. But pollution isn't the only cause of environmental degradation, and even if emissions externalities are completely absent the natural environment can still be destroyed and wasted by simple misuse. To address this issue this chapter examines what constitutes efficient management of natural environmental resources, beginning in this section with renewable natural resources.

Renewable natural resources are those natural resources which grow (i.e. renew) over time, such as fish stocks which grow in the sea, or trees which grow on a piece of land. The rate of population growth of natural resources is often modelled using a logistic function, and this predicts that the growth rate will increase over time, but then is forced into a decline as the population size rises. This log function trend of rising then declining growth makes intuitive sense, and at first when a part of the sea has few fish or a piece of land has few trees there is the potential resources and living space for ever increasing growth in numbers. But as the space in an area of the sea or on a piece of land is taken up there simply isn't enough resources and room for the population of fish or trees respectively to keep growing at any ever increasing rate, and the maximum possible growth rate of the population, known as the maximum sustainable yield, is reached. After that maximum sustainable yield point the rate of growth of a population will decline due to limited resources, until eventually there is no room for any additional fish to survive in a part of the sea or for additional trees to survive on a piece of land, and the growth rate will fall to zero. And the population level where the growth rate falls to zero is the upper bound of the population size, the maximum possible size that the population can grow to before an area of the sea can't sustain any more fish or a piece of land cannot sustain any more trees.

An image can make the idea of logistic growth clearer, and the following diagram shows an example of a logistic function for population growth. MSY stands for the maximum sustainable yield and represents the maximum possible rate of growth in the population, which occurs at point X in the diagram. The corresponding population size for this maximum sustainable yield is denoted by S_{MSY}, and the maximum possible population size in the image (when growth has declined to zero) is denoted as S_{MAX}.

A logistic function for population growth

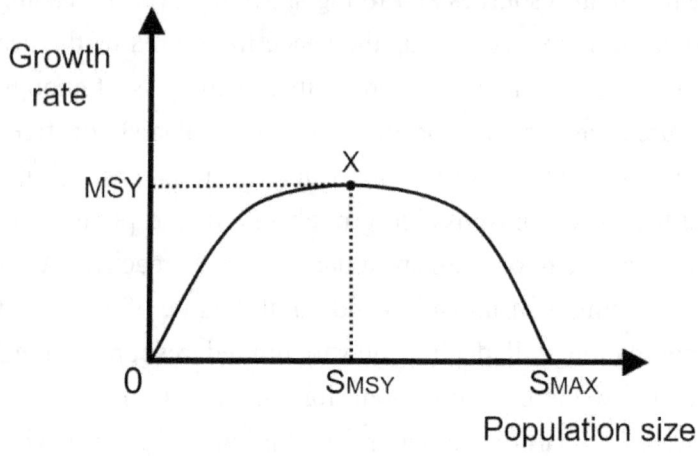

With the likely population growth rate and reproductive capacity of renewable natural resources explained the next question is how they should be harvested, and what would constitute efficient management of the natural resources. Management of natural resources involves two aspects: the natural availability of those natural resources (i.e. the growth rate), and the rate at which humans use up those natural resources (i.e. the harvesting magnitude). If the growth rate of natural resources is denoted by the letter G, and the magnitude of the harvest collected is denoted by the letter H, then the rate of change in the size (S) of the population of resources over time (t) can be written as G – H. That is to say that the population growth rate minus the magnitude of harvest gives the rate of change in the size of the population over time, and derivative $dS/dt = G - H$.

If $G = H$ and the growth rate equals the harvesting magnitude then the rate of change in the population size over time is zero, and the stock of fish or trees will remain the same. In this situation the level of growth will be sustainable and the level of harvesting is sustainable, and there will be a sustainable yield and a steady stock of resources available for harvest over time. For example, if there was 100,000 fish in an area of the sea, with a population growth rate of 20% per year, and fishermen harvest 20% of the fish stocks per year, then the fish population of that area of the sea will equal 100,000 (starting population) + 20,000 (growth rate of 20% or 0.2 * 100,000 starting population) − 20,000 (harvesting magnitude of 20% or 0.2 * 100,000 starting population) = 100,000. Therefore every year the fish population will remain at 100,000 and harvests will be sustainable, with no threat of the natural resources being exhausted.

If $G > H$ and the growth rate of the population is greater than the harvesting magnitude then fishermen are harvesting less resources than they could. For example, if the starting population of fish in an area of the seas was again 100,000 and the annual growth rate was again 20% (20,000 fish), but the annual harvesting rate was only 10% (10,000 fish), then after one year the fish population would be 100,000 + 20,000 − 10,000 = 110,000. Although the

67

harvesting rate in this example is also sustainable, the 10,000 or 10% increase in the fish population represents the additional amount of fish resources that fishermen could have taken from the sea without depleting the stock of natural resources, and it could therefore be seen as a lost opportunity and a loss to the harvesters.

But if $G < H$ and the growth rate of the population is less than the harvesting magnitude then fisherman are taking too many fish from the sea, and fish stocks will eventually be completely depleted. For example, if there were 100,000 fish in an area of the sea, a 10% annual growth rate (10,000 fish) but a 20% annual harvesting rate (20,000) fish, then after one year the fish population would be $100,000 + 10,000 - 20,000 = 90,000$. This 10% loss in the fish population may represent a gain for the harvesters in the short-run as more fish are collected, but in time if this harvesting trend is maintained there wouldn't be any fish to harvest at all and it would therefore represent a major loss. A harvesting magnitude greater than the population growth rate simply isn't sustainable.

The magnitude and size of the harvest is the deciding factor in whether or not essential renewable natural resources are sustained indefinitely or if they will eventually be exhausted. And the harvest (H) is determined by two factors: the population stock size (S) and the effort (E) put into harvesting: $H = H(E, S)$. As the relationship between the population stock and effort is clearly a direct one, with the harvest not possible without both a stock to harvest and effort undertaken to harvest it, the harvest can be denoted as the product of the population stock and the harvesters' effort: $H = ES$. The higher the stock or the effort the greater the harvest will be, and with harvesters having little control over the starting population stock of natural resources it will be their effort that ultimately determines the harvest. Effort will clearly also determine the size of the remaining population stock, for example a large (effort driven) harvest results in a smaller stock of fish left in the sea, and a smaller (effort driven) harvest results in a larger stock of fish left in the sea. And with the population stock in turn linked to the prospects for growth (i.e. a logistic growth function as just explained), it can also be said that growth (G) is the product of effort (E) and the population stock (S): $G = ES$.

Another diagram can make the above explanation clearer, and the following diagram replicates the last image of population size (S) against growth rate (G), but with several additional features. The vertical axis now also represents the harvest magnitude (H), with the equilibrium point X now representing both the maximum sustainable yield (MSY) and the maximum sustainable harvest (MSH), which is the largest harvest that could be regularly collected without eventually exhausting natural resources stocks. Also added in this diagram are two $H = ES$ lines, E_1S and E_2S, which show how different combinations of effort and population stock size result in different levels of resulting harvest. Line E_1S shows one fixed level of effort (E_1), and a move rightwards in the diagram shows the effects of combining this unchanging level of effort with an ever greater stock size, and the result is a greater harvest as the E_1S line moves upwards. As S increases along the E_1S line, H also increases, even though effort is kept unchanged.

Effort, size of stock, and harvests

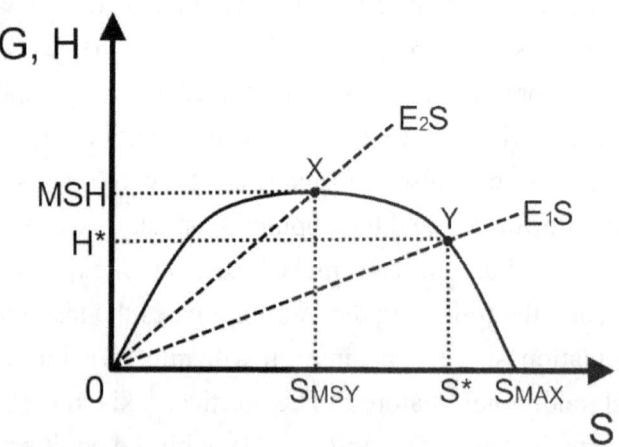

If harvesters only put in an E_1 level of effort into their harvesting then the equilibrium point would be point Y, with a population stock size of S* and resulting harvest at level H*. At this point the $E_1S = H$ harvest line crosses the growth curve (G) introduced in the previous diagram, and therefore at this point $E_1S = H = G$. This satisfies the $G = H$ criteria where the growth rate equals the harvest magnitude for a sustainable yield as explained earlier, and represents a sustainable harvest where the resources will be able to renew themselves for indefinite future harvests. Any point along line E_1S within the growth curve area (i.e. to the left of point Y on line E_1S with a lower stock size) is also sustainable, but sees the harvest magnitude less than the growth rate $(G > H)$ and therefore represents a lost opportunity in terms of the resources collected. Any point along line E_1S outside the growth rate curve (i.e. to the right of point Y on line E_1S with a greater stock size) sees the harvest magnitude greater than the growth rate $(G < H)$ which is not sustainable, and would see the depletion of all renewable natural resources in the long-run. And therefore point Y is the equilibrium for an E_1 effort level.

Line E_2S shows the situation where harvesters put in a higher E_2 amount of effort, with effort fixed at this level while the population stock size (S) changes with a move along the E_2S line. As the diagram shows, the higher effort of line E_2S compared to line E_1S ensures that the former is steeper, with line E_2S generating a visibly higher harvest (H) than line E_1S for every level of population stock size (S). The equilibrium point for line E_2S is point X, and this generates the maximum sustainable harvest (MSH) and yield available for either of the two effort levels E_1 or E_2 here, with a corresponding population stock size at S_{MSY}.

Point X is the equilibrium for an E_2 effort level because at this point the $E_2S = H$ line crosses the growth curve (G), to fulfil the $G = H$ criteria needed for a sustainable yield and harvest. Any point along line E_2S within the growth curve (i.e. left of point X on line E_2S) is also sustainable but is non-optimal, as it sees the harvest magnitude below the growth rate ($G > H$) and the harvest is lower than could have been taken without consequence. But any point along line E_2S outside the growth curve (i.e. right of point X on the E_2S line) is not sustainable, as it involves the harvest magnitude exceeding the growth rate ($G < H$), which would deplete and ultimately exhaust the stock of natural resources, making future harvests impossible.

The analysis so far has shown that the more effort that is put into harvesting the greater the harvest will be. However, the size of the harvest is not necessarily the driving factor in determining the level of effort which will be exerted. As usual in economics it is profitability which drives peoples' decisions in environmental economics, and therefore the most optimal harvest will be the most profitable one, given existing harvesting technology. Profitability is determined by revenue against costs, with the harvest itself generating revenue after harvested resources are sold, while the effort exerted to secure the harvest incurs costs. The following diagram looks more at the relationship between costs and revenue, by showing more examples of how changing the effort level (which incurs costs) can affect the size of the harvest (which determines revenue).

Changing effort and resulting harvests

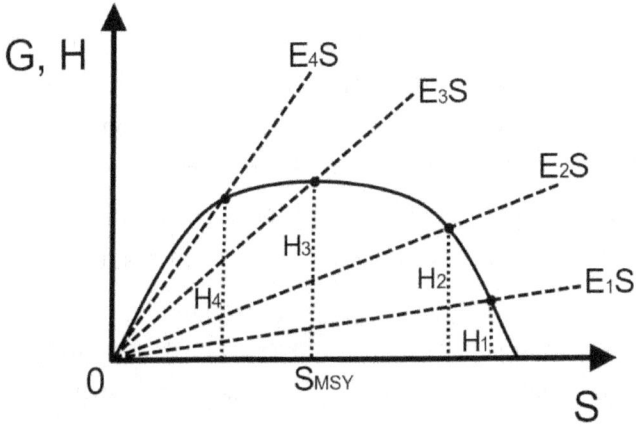

Effort level E_1S and higher effort level E_2S are repeated from the last diagram, but are now renamed E_2S and E_3S respectively, as two additional effort levels have also been added. A new effort level lower than the earlier two, E_1, has been added to the analysis, and combinations of this fixed lower effort level with changing levels of stock size (S) are given with new line E_1S. The second new effort level added to the analysis, effort level E_4, is a greater effort level than any of the others, and line E_4S combines this fixed higher effort level with various different stock sizes (S). Each of the four different effort levels, E_1, E_2, E_3, and E_4, and the four different H = ES harvest possibilities which result, E_1S, E_2S, E_3S, and E_4S, are associated with four different optimal harvests respectively, marked H_1, H_2, H_3 and H_4 and associated with the adjacent dotted lines. And as explained in the previous diagram, each of these optimal harvests occurs where the respective ES effort multiplied by stock size line crosses the growth curve. At any other point on an ES line the harvest is either too small and represents a missed opportunity to collect more resources, or the harvest is too large and will see the depletion of natural resources in the long-run.

The diagram reveals that increasing effort (and costs) doesn't necessarily always increase the size of the sustainable harvest (and revenue). While increasing effort from E_1 to E_2, and then from E_2 to E_3 does increase the optimal harvest, as clear by the growth curve being cut at a higher point, increasing effort further from E_3 to E_4 reduces the size of the harvest, with line E_4S clearly cutting the growth curve at a lower point and giving a smaller sustainable harvest than line E_3S. But increasing effort levels always reduces the stock size, and although not marked on the diagram a zero effort level (i.e. E_0) would coincide with a maximum possible population stock size (S_{MAX}) where the growth curve has declined to zero. And all of this information on the relationship between effort and harvest can be put into a more accessible form in another diagram, which plots worker effort against harvest size directly, as a precursor to showing how the total costs of effort matches up against the total revenue of harvests. The next diagram can be referred to as an effort-harvest function.

Effort-harvest function

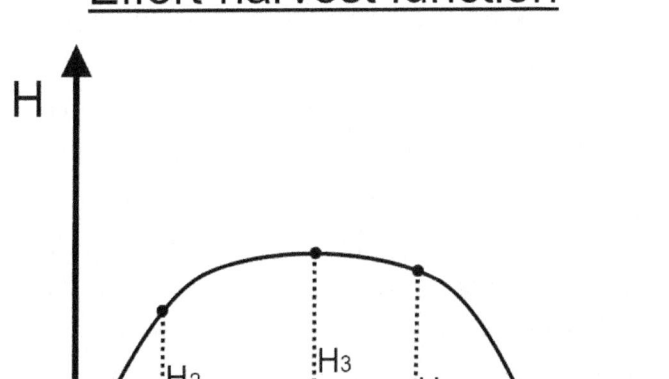

Note that effort rises from left to right in this effort-harvest function, as is usual in economic diagrams, as opposed to the more unusual situation shown in the previous two diagrams where effort increased from right to left instead. With a symmetric growth curve the effort-harvest function here is an exact mirror image of the last diagram in terms of the position of optimal harvests on the growth curve.

And with this effort-harvest function a detailed analysis of the costs and revenue associated with different harvesting choices can now take place, to reveal the most profitable effort-harvest combination which will ultimately come to pass as the chosen optimal sustainable harvest. The profitability (π) of a harvest is found by subtracting the total costs (TC) of that harvest from the total revenue (TR) associated with that harvest, $\pi = TR - TC$. The total revenue from a harvest is found by multiplying the size of the harvest (H) by the price (p) that the harvested resources can then be sold on at, $TR = pH$. And the total cost of a harvest is found by multiplying the effort exerted by harvesting workers (E) by the wage (w) workers demand to exert that effort, $TC = wE$, assuming that effort (i.e. labour) is the only production factor for harvesting.

With wages assumed to be constant, the only factor determining the shape of the total cost function would be effort, and therefore the TC total cost function will be a straight line increasing with effort, and with slope w. And with the price a harvest can be sold at also assumed constant, the only factor determining the shape of the TR total revenue function would be the size of the harvest. It has already been determined that the only harvests under consideration are those which are optimal sustainable harvests, where $H = G$ the growth rate. All other harvests are either missed opportunities (H < G), or are unsustainable harvest and would deplete the ability of natural resources to renew themselves (H > G). All optimal harvests occur on the growth curve, and therefore the growth curve could be considered a total revenue curve if price p = 1 is assumed for simplicity. If p doesn't equal 1 the following analysis and conclusions would still apply, but the total revenue TR function (price p multiplied by optimal harvest H) would be situated above or below the growth curve.

The following diagram is the effort-harvest function again, but with the total revenue and total cost functions just discussed now added. Effort levels E_1, E_2, E_3, and E_4 have been replicated from the previous diagram, but with the highest effort level E_4 now redrawn a little further to the right to make this diagram and the analysis clearer. TC = wE is the total cost line, with slope w (constant wages) and rising with effort E. TR = pH is the total revenue curve, assuming constant prices (at p = 1 here) where only optimal harvests (H = G) are considered. There are two possible outcomes in this diagram, point X and point Y, and which comes to pass depends upon whether or not there are well-allocated property rights.

In the scenario where property rights haven't yet been assigned, or where they are not properly enforced, it is reasonable to assume that a large number of people will attempt to harvest renewable natural resources to then sell on for revenue. If an area of the sea didn't have property rights assigned to it, for example, a significant number of fishermen may all compete to catch as many fish as they can, and together they may exert a high level of effort in an attempt to secure a greater harvest and higher revenue. This ever greater effort pushes the harvesters rightwards along the optimal harvest curve, which is also the growth and total revenue TR curve, up to effort level E_4 in the diagram, the highest level of effort labelled in the diagram.

Costs, revenue, and profits, with and without property rights

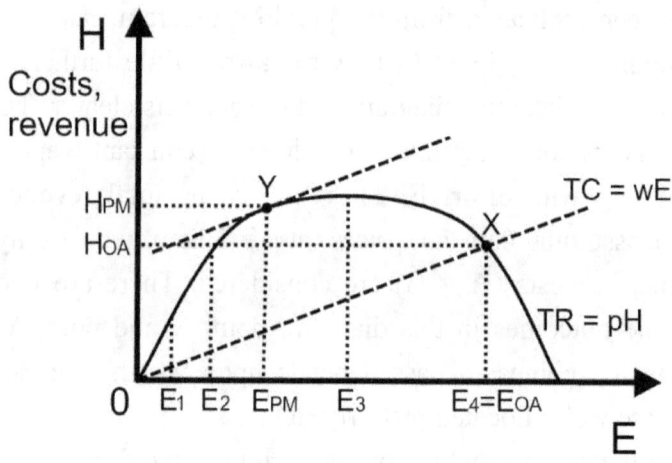

This E_4 effort level is labelled E_{OA} as it is the effort level which will come to pass under open access (OA) and a lack of property rights. At this point the total revenue (TR) and total costs (TC) associated with exerting effort to secure a harvest are equal, $TR = TC$, and there is no additional revenue available to chase without also incurring costs which would incur a loss, which harvesters wouldn't accept. In other words, any effort level above E_4 sees the profit level $\pi = TR - TC$ turn into a negative value as TC exceeds TR, and therefore those harvesting will stop putting in effort at this point. But under open access, without property rights, peoples' scramble to get revenue has pushed them to a point where they put too much effort into harvesting. They don't stop until all profits are gone and they just cut even with profit of $\pi = TR - TC = 0$ at point X, with effort level E_{OA} and a harvest of size H_{OA}. This situation where common or open access to shared resources results in a worse situation for all concerned, as individuals acting rationally in their own independent self-interest to acquire as many resources as possible end up depleting the resources for all parties, and damaging the common good, is known as the 'tragedy of the commons'.

If property rights do exist however then the analysis changes completely. Instead of a large and potentially limitless number of harvesters collecting resources and chasing revenue until all profits are gone there will only be a limited amount of harvesting undertaken, by those who hold the property rights or on their behalf. By holding the exclusive property rights to harvest harvesters are free to focus on their goal of profit maximization, and don't have to worry about others exerting too much effort and harvesting too much to ruin this plan. Profit maximization occurs in the diagram at the point where total revenue TR exceeds total costs TC by the greatest amount. This occurs at point Y, and a parallel line is drawn from the TC line to highlight this fact and make it clearer. Profit maximization point Y requires effort level E_{PM} (which stands for profit maximization), a new effort level between established E_2 and E_3 levels, and generates a harvest of size H_{PM}.

While the maximum sustainable harvest (MSH) and yield (MSY) was earlier identified as occurring with effort level E_3, right in the middle of the growth curve, the optimal private harvesting outcomes where harvesters pursue profits are different, both in the case with property rights and without them. Without property rights and with open access to renewable natural resources too many harvesters will put in too much effort at $E_4 = E_{OA}$, and reduce the stock level of renewable natural resources (see the previous 'changing effort and resulting harvests' diagram to see how increasing effort always reduces the population stock size, even though it may not always mean a greater harvest). Therefore not only is open access to renewable natural resources bad as a private solution, as it generates zero profit, it is also bad as a social solution to environmental management. It will result in a lower stock of natural resources than if the private profit motive had been ignored, and the focus had been on securing as big a harvest as possible to meet natural community needs instead.

With property rights assigned to private profit-seeking harvesters there will be fewer harvesters and less effort exerted, and individuals will be able to select the profit maximizing level of effort E_{PM}. And not only is this better for private individuals as it generates the maximum possible profit, it is also better as a social solution to environmental management, as less effort exerted in harvesting means there will be a greater stock of renewable natural resources remaining.

In conclusion, the efficient management of renewable resources and the protection of a large stock of natural resources can best be achieved using property rights, and simply allowing individuals to follow their natural profit maximization motives. There therefore isn't necessarily any need for government intervention in order to efficiently manage renewable natural resources. However, there may be a natural absence of property rights, or property rights which aren't properly enforced, in areas such as fishing in the sea, and in this scenario government intervention to develop or strongly enforce property rights may be required to achieve a better social (and also private) solution.

In those scenarios where open access is the norm with renewable natural resources, and government is unable to allocate or enforce property rights to stop it, the government may require a different strategy. While open access will naturally result in more effort by harvesters and a resulting lower resource stock level, it wouldn't threaten to completely deplete stocks unless worker effort had a zero cost (causing limitless harvesting effort) and harvest magnitude consistently exceeded the growth rate of stocks over time. And therefore government strategy to combat the risks associated with this inefficient open access should target these areas. They may make technical restrictions and ban fishing nets which make it easy to effortlessly catch large amounts of fish, put taxes on fishing time or on catches, or require fishermen to hold tradable catch permits before they are allowed to fish, all of which raise the cost of exerting harvesting effort. Or alternatively government may put restrictions on the amount of time that fishermen may fish, or the quantity of fish which can be harvested, both of which would serve to reduce the risk that harvests would consistently exceed fish population stock growth rates.

There are some caveats to this analysis however, and it has been implicitly assumed that externalities are not present. But if externalities are present then they would also need to be addressed, possibly using the methods put forward in the pollution control sections. All of the discussion here has also only focused on a static analysis of resource management, and adding the dynamic intertemporal dimension and factoring in changes over time adds the possibility for changing wages, changing resource prices, and the need to discount future cash flows due to the time value of money. In the absence of property rights these issues have the potential to change results considerably, and add further challenges to government and its task of protecting renewable natural resources.

4.2 Non-Renewable Natural Resources

The last section explored how to efficiently manage renewable natural resources such as fish in the sea, or trees in a forest on land, but not all natural resources are renewable. Resources such as fossil fuels coal and oil can take millions of years of time to form, and for all intents and purposes they are therefore non-renewable. And the efficient management of these resources is therefore a very different challenge to that examined in the last section.

The socially optimal extraction of non-renewable natural resources from the earth and sea will require for the present value of discounted social welfare to be maximized, given the constraint that all of the existing non-renewable natural resources will be extracted and used by the end of the period in question. In other words, the socially optimal use of non-renewable resources requires that they are efficiently used to support social welfare (i.e. consumption and production) over time. And the private optimal extraction of non-renewable natural resources will require for the present value of discounted profits to be maximized, given the constraint that all of the existing non-renewable natural resources will be extracted by the end of the period in question. In other words, the private optimal use of non-renewable resources requires that they are efficiently used to generate profits over time.

With assigned and enforced property rights, and in the absence of market failures, the socially optimal extraction path will coincide with the private profit-maximizing optimal extraction path. The logic behind this is that the socially optimal extraction schedule is the one which offers the highest social welfare to citizens, and generates the greatest social value. Therefore, in the absence of market failure, this will be recognized by markets and it will also have the highest market value. As the social optimal extraction path has the highest market value it will generate the greatest profit, and it is therefore the profit-maximizing private optimal extraction path too, as long as assigned and enforced property rights exist. Without property rights there will be too many profit-seeking resource harvesters, all competing to extract limited resources before others take them, which will drive profits to zero and ensure profit-maximization is missed (as shown in the last section).

The decision on the (both social and private) optimal extraction rate is an intertemporal question, as a higher extraction rate in the present enforces a lower extraction rate in the future (as the stock of non-renewable resources will have been reduced), while a lower extraction rate in the present allows a higher rate in the future. And therefore a determining factor in extraction is the extent to which people in the present care for the future, and whether they prefer to consume returns from resources today, or invest in resources today so that they will be available for themselves in old age or for their children to consume in the future. However, there is an opportunity cost associated with delaying the extraction of resources until the future, and it means that resources can't be sold today and the revenue invested in a bank to generate interest and revenue for the future.

A discount rate is usually used to measure the extent to which people care for the future relative to the present, and as the name suggests this discounts the value of gains (profits or social welfare gains) expected in the future by a certain percentage rate. This discounting process turns forecasted future gains into present day gains which then allows a numerical comparison with other present day gains, to determine whether people are better off consuming now, or instead investing to consume in the future. A higher discount rate (e.g. 10% to 20%) for future resource gains suggests the future is valued less than the present, and a relatively higher extraction rate would be expected today than in the future. But a low discount rate (e.g. 1% to 5%) for future resource gains suggests the opposite, and that the future is valued higher than the present, and a relatively lower extraction rate would be expected today than in the future. As suggested in the last paragraph, the interest rate may often be used as the discount rate.

Economist Hotelling came up with a model to determine the optimal allocation of resources over time, and the optimal (both social welfare maximizing and private profit-maximizing) extraction path for non-renewable natural resources. According to his theory, 'an optimal extraction path will emerge when the rate of growth in the price of the resource is equal to the social discount rate, assuming that resources can be extracted at no cost'. As the rate of growth adjusts present values to future values, and the discount rate adjusts future values to present values, while prices relate to private profit-maximizing goals, and the social discount rate relates to the social, Hotelling's theory can be simplified further. It basically states that the optimal extraction rate exists when: growth rate = discount rate, and private gains = social gains. It has already been noted that the private and social optimal extraction rate (for private and social gains) will be equal with the existence of property rights and no market failure causing externalities. Therefore Hotelling's model only requires growth and discount rates to be equal.

The rate of growth of a price over a period of time can be found by subtracting the current price at the start of the time period ($p0$) from the price at the period end (pT), and then dividing by the price at the start of the period ($p0$), growth rate = (pT – $p0$) / $p0$. And with the social discount rate (r), the rate at which future social gains are discounted before being compared with current social gains, Hotelling's model for optimal extraction is:

$$(pT - p0) / p0 = r$$

If the price growth rate exceeds the discount rate, with $(pT - p0) / p0 > r$, then the extraction rate is too high and resources are being used up too quickly, causing scarcity and pushing up prices too high. More resources should be left in the ground to let them grow in value over time. If the growth rate is less than the discount rate, $(pT - p0) / p0 < r$, then the extraction rate is too low and resources are being used up too slowly, causing an excess and lowering prices as a result. More resources should be extracted now before they decline in value. Only if the price growth rate equals the discount rate will the extraction rate and the allocation of resources over time be optimal.

The equation above can be rearranged step by step to rewrite it in terms of pT, for an important conclusion:

$$(pT - p0) / p0 = r$$
$$pT - p0 = r * p0$$
$$pT = (r * p0) + p0$$
$$pT = p0 (1 + r)$$

This last line of $pT = p0 (1 + r)$ is simply a rearrangement of Hotelling's theory for optimal non-renewable natural resource extraction, and it reveals that the 'optimal extraction occurs when future prices are equal to current prices after accounting for the discount rate'. In other words 'the optimal resource allocation and extraction rate will occur when discounted prices are constant over time'. As the growth rate in prices is often referred to as marginal revenue, and rate of interest is typically used as the discount rate, the Hotelling rule is often referred to as 'optimal resource allocation and extraction rate will occur when marginal revenue increases at the rate of interest'.

The following diagram illustrates Hotelling's rule in visual form. It appears complicated, but it can be easily understood if the four quadrants are looked at in turn.

The bottom-left quadrant shows the price path of the non-renewable natural resource, with time (t) on the vertical axis and the price over time (p(t)) on the horizontal axis. The bottom-left of the price path in the bottom left quadrant, with the highest price (most leftward point) on the price path and the furthest ahead in time (t), represents the price of the resource at the end of the time period when all of the resource has been extracted. A dotted line links this up to the horizontal axis where it is labelled as pT accordingly. The other end of the price path, labelled p0, represents the price of the resource at the start of the time period before any of the resource has been extracted, and it is linked with a zero value on the vertical time axis, and the lowest p(t) value on the price path.

In the upper-left quadrant there is a demand curve with quantity of resources demanded over time (q(t)) plotted against resource price (p(t)). The upper-left quadrant represents the social discounting process which makes end prices equal to current prices, with the slope indicating the discount rate. Price pT (end price) from the bottom-left quadrant corresponds to the start of the demand curve with a zero quantity demanded value, while price p0 (current price) also connects to the demand curve via a dotted line from the bottom-left quadrant, with the quantity demanded the maximum available quantity of resources.

The upper-right quadrant shows the extraction path of natural resources, with quantity of resources (q(t)) against time. And this optimal extraction path begins where the price path (growth in prices) equals the slope of the demand curve (social discount rate). The total stock of non-renewable natural resources is labelled within the area of this extraction path. The maximum stock and highest q(t) value on the vertical axis on the upper-right quadrant occurs before any extraction has begun, with a zero value on the horizontal time axis. This point is linked with a dotted line to the upper-left quadrant and the maximum quantity of resources demanded, given the bottom-left quadrant's current price p0. The other end of the extraction path in the upper-right quadrant sees all non-renewable resources extracted, with a zero value on the q(t) axis, and an end of the time period T value on the time axis.

Hotelling's rule

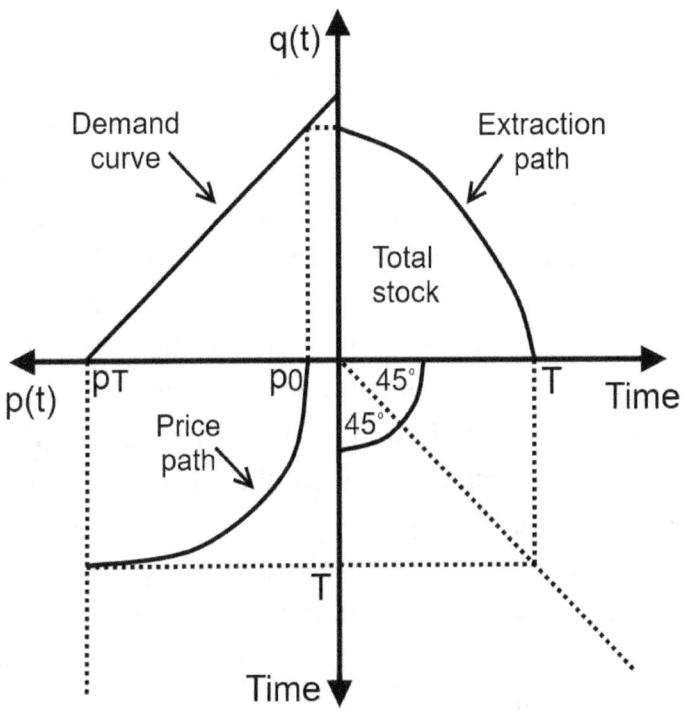

Finally, the bottom-right quadrant simply connects the upper-right and bottom-left quadrants using time. Time T in the upper-right quadrant, the end of the non-renewable natural resources lifespan where all resources have been extracted, is connected with a dotted line to time T and then on to price pT (end price) in the bottom-left quadrant. This is to show that the end of the non-renewable resources (in the top-right quadrant) occurs at the same time (time T) as the end price pT (bottom-left quadrant), with the two 45 degree angles in the time bottom-right quadrant there to show that the bottom-left and upper-right quadrants are mirror images of each other in terms of time.

However, the ideas in this diagram and Hotelling's rule in general may not hold up in practice. In practice there may be difficulties in determining the social discount rate (r) which makes future prices and current prices equal and reflects the extent to which people in the present care for the future. And even if a discounting rate can be determined (e.g. the rate of interest), it may be difficult equating the growth in prices (marginal revenue) with it for an optimal extraction, due to the inherent instability, fluctuations and risk in prices.

The Hotelling rule just explained had one central assumption, that resource extraction costs were zero, and it operates on this basis. If there are extraction costs, as there most likely will be in practice, then this Hotelling rule will no longer work. The addition of extraction costs will affect the profitability of a private profit-maximizing harvester, and with private and social optimal extraction rates equal (assuming property rights and no market failure as noted earlier) it will also affect social welfare. Therefore the Hotelling rule will need to be amended into a modified Hotelling rule in the presence of resource extraction costs. The modified Hotelling rule states that 'the optimal allocation of resources and optimal extraction rate occurs when the social discount rate equals the growth rate of prices, minus the value of the marginal costs of the extraction'. Or in other words the rule is that 'the optimal extraction occurs where net marginal revenue increases at the rate of interest'. This modified Hotelling rule is given by the following formula:

$$(M\pi T - M\pi 0) / M\pi 0 = r$$

This is very similar to the original Hotelling formula, the only difference being that marginal (extraction) costs are now accounted for, as prices (p) are replaced by marginal profit ($M\pi$), where $M\pi = p - MC$, with 'M' standing for marginal, 'π' for profit, and 'MC' for marginal costs. And while in the original Hotelling rule the optimal allocation and extraction rate of resources over time occurred when discounted prices are equal over time, with the modified Hotelling rule 'the optimal allocation and extraction rate of resources occurs when discounted prices are equal to discounted marginal extraction costs'.

With the original Hotelling rule the determining factors in the optimal extraction and allocation rate were only the growth rate of prices, and the discount rate, but the modified Hotelling rule also has marginal extraction costs as a determining factor. These marginal extraction costs are positively correlated with the cost of extraction inputs (such as worker wage costs), and with the extraction rate, but marginal extraction costs are negatively correlated with the amount of non-renewable natural resources reserves remaining (due to scarcity and the laws of supply and demand). As all of these three variables can be affected by technological progress there is a strong likelihood that the marginal cost of extraction will change over time with natural advances in technology, if the modified Hotelling rule is accurate, and with it the optimal allocation and extraction rate.

The marginal cost of extraction in the modified Hotelling rule may be reduced by improved technology creating more efficient machinery and reducing the need for expensive workers, to lower the cost of extraction inputs. Or technological advances may make it feasible to extract previously untapped stocks of non-renewable natural resources (as the expansion of fracking has shown), essentially adding to the stock of natural resources and lowering marginal extraction costs due to greater supply and overabundance. Or perhaps technology may create alternatives to fossil fuels which make society less reliant on non-renewable natural resources, thereby reducing the extraction rate and with it the marginal cost of extraction. Alternatively, marginal extraction costs may rise due to technology facilitating more efficient extraction, which pushes up the extraction rate and reduces the stock of resources, to push up prices via a scarcity effect.

5 Policy Valuation and Cost-Benefit Analysis

The previous chapters have focussed on the big environmental economics issues of how to control pollution, and how to efficiently manage both renewable and non-renewable natural resources. But the environmental issues which society or government faces are often of a smaller and more local nature, such as where to build new roads to best balance both efficiency and environmental needs. This chapter examines how these day to day issues are dealt with in practice, through environmental policy valuation techniques and cost-benefit analysis.

Before an environmental project is given the go-ahead it will be assessed for its economic, environmental and social efficiency. This process will evaluate whether the project would offer a Pareto improvement and increase Pareto efficiency, by offering an overall gain to social welfare where those benefiting from the project could theoretically afford to compensate the losers from the project and still end up better than before. This policy valuation can be conducted using cost-benefit analysis, where the benefits (gains) and costs (losses) of the proposed project are determined then compared. The stages of cost-benefit analysis (CBA) are as follows:

1. Project definition

First, the proposed project is defined. This involves deciding exactly what is planned, whose welfare would be affected, and how long the project is planned to last. For example, the project may be decided as the building of new bypass road through a rural area in an attempt to reduce traffic problems for road users. The new road may be expected to last for twenty years, before significant repair or change is required. And those having their welfare affected would be those directly involved with the project, the drivers using the new road, and those who currently use the rural area which would be changed significantly by the creation of the bypass.

2. Identify physical impacts of project

The second step identifies the resource allocation and physical impacts associated with the project. For example, a new bypass project would affect the driving time for those drivers using the new roads (its stated purpose), require labour hours resources from workers to build it, and have a physical impact on the air quality of the area. Once the likely physical impacts have been identified they would be divided into two separate columns, one noting the predicted benefits or advantages associated with the project, the other noting the likely costs or disadvantages.

For example, the benefits/advantages/gains resulting from the completion of a bypass road project to reduce traffic may include time savings for drivers, a reduction in the number of accidents (due to less traffic) on alternative nearby roads, and an improved sound quality (due to less traffic) and air quality (less traffic reduces pollution emissions) for those living by alternative nearby roads.

The costs/disadvantages/losses resulting from the completion of a new bypass project through a rural area may include a reduction in the quality of the natural landscape and aesthetic value, a loss of a habitat for flora and fauna, a loss of use value for those who had utilised the rural area (e.g. for walking), and increased sound and air pollution with a resultant decrease in property values for those living in the area of the new bypass.

3. Value the physical impacts of project

With the likely physical impacts of a project identified the third step is the numerical valuation of these impacts. For example, the number of drivers' labour hours expected to be saved by the bypass would be determined, with the extent to which flora and fauna would be damaged by pollution, the expected reduction in property values near the new bypass, and the extent to which people would miss the soon to be bulldozed rural landscape and walk area.

With numerical values assigned to the physical impacts of a project monetary values could be determined. The ideal goal would be to determine monetary values in the form of the marginal social benefits (MSB) of a project, against the marginal social costs (MSC) of a project, in market prices or in estimate shadow prices if true market prices were impossible to determine. Determining the MSB and MSC of a project in market prices would not only reveal whether or not the project was efficient and should proceed (i.e. if benefits exceed costs), but the marginal nature of the monetary values could also reveal the changes to the project required to reach the equilibrium and most efficient point, where MSB = MSC. But before the marginal social benefits and marginal social costs of a project are determined the constituent parts of a project must all be valued. There are three main types of valuation approaches which can be used to achieve this goal. These are stated preference, revealed preference, and production function approaches.

Stated preference approaches

The Contingent Valuation Method (CVM) is a stated preference approach which attempts to create a market for the environment by asking people how they value the environment. CVM may involve an inquiry into respondents' Willingness to Pay (WTP), and the maximum amount of money they were willing to pay to prevent environmental damage to a part of the environment. Or it may question peoples' Willingness to Accept (WTA), and the minimum monetary compensation it would take for them to accept environmental damage without complaint.

The Choice Experiments Method is another stated preference approach of valuation, and this method follows the characteristics theory of value, which sees value and demand as originating from specific attributes and characteristics of a good, rather than the good itself. In the choice experiments method the main attributes related to the landscape will be determined and then presented to a focus group, which will be asked to choose their preference between a statistically designed bundle of attributes and a status quo alternative. With cost included as an attribute, and with the method repeated for a range of different bundles with alternative attributes, peoples' willingness to pay can be determined and with it their valuation of the environment.

Contingent Ranking is also a characteristics theory of value approach to valuation. It sees different bundles of attributes presented to respondents, with a cost attached to each bundle. The respondents then rank the bundles of attributes from their most preferred to their least preferred, and this reveals their valuation of environmental features.

Revealed preference approaches

The Hedonic Pricing Method (HPM) is a revealed preference method of valuation. It shares the characteristics theory of value as the last two methods, but hedonic pricing is focused entirely on issues relating to housing prices. HPM attributes include features of houses (age, number of bedrooms, etc.) and then determine how changes in environmental air quality, noise, or proximity to waste sits affect house prices. This HPM method has the advantage that house price market data is readily available to analyse, but the disadvantage that it can't assess any environmental projects which aren't close to property.

The Travel Cost Method (TCM) observes or surveys the expenditure people spend, such as time and money, on travelling to a location. This reveals the demand curve for a specific environmental location, which can be used to find the total value and the consumer surplus (the difference between what consumers are willing to pay and what they actually have to pay) associated with the area.

Production function approaches

A Dose-Response model is a production function model, and as the name suggests it involves giving a dose of pollution to the environment to see its physical response. The method is typically used to study the effects of air pollutants on crops and forests, and the response is estimated using special models to evaluate the net effects on output, consumer surplus, and producers' profit.

4. Discounting

After the physical impacts of a project have been valued in terms of monetary costs and benefits, using one or several of the valuation approaches just explained, the next and fourth step is to apply discounting. Monetary costs or benefits forecasted for the future must be discounted according to the principle of the time value of money, where benefits are less valuable and costs are less damaging the further into the future they are expected. To convert future costs and benefits into current or present values, to allow an accurate comparison over time, a discount rate must be used. A commonly used discount rate to discount future money flows is the risk-free rate of interest, as this shows how much more money could be reliably expected over time if it was invested in a bank, essentially turning present values into future values. To turn forecasted future monetary values (costs and benefits) into present day cost and benefit values the following formula is used, where r is the expected discount rate, and t the number of time periods (i.e. no. of years if interest is paid annually): Present value = future value $[(1 + r)^{-t}]$.

5. Net present value test

With future values discounted into present values the next and fifth step is to compare the sum ($\sum$) of discounted benefits (Bt) or gains, $\sum Bt \left[(1 + r)^{-t}\right]$, with the sum of discounted costs (Ct) or losses, $\sum Ct \left[(1 + r)^{-t}\right]$. Subtracting the sum of discounted costs from the sum of discounted benefits gives the net present value (NPV) of all project cash flows, $NPV = \sum Bt \left[(1 + r)^{-t}\right] - \sum Ct \left[(1 + r)^{-t}\right]$. If the NPV is positive the project generates a net benefit, and it is economically efficient and will generate an improvement in social welfare, and should therefore proceed. If the NPV is zero or if there is a negative NPV then the project will not generate a net benefit and should not proceed.

6. Sensitivity analysis

The sixth and final step in cost-benefit analysis tests for the effects of changes in data or the discount rate, to ensure the NPV will remain positive if there are some small and theoretically possible deviations from expectations. If the NPV is still positive after small changes to project lifespan, input or output costs, quantities, and qualities, or the discount rate, then the project can proceed as planned.